# AT THE CORNER OF BITTER & SWEET

CHOOSING BEAUTY IN LIFE'S PAINFUL PLACES

AMY JOY STOUT

Scripture quotations are taken from the Holy Bible, New International Version, NIV. Copyright © 1973, 1978, 1984, 2011 by Biblica, Inc.

Published by His Beloved Printing Press

Cover Photo by Drew Stout Photography

Cover Letter Art by Alexis Stout

Cover Design by L. Hensley (www.lhensley.com)

Editing & Formatting by Halcyon Books (www.halcyonbooks.biz)

Paperback ISBN 978-1-7333221-1-9

*To my daughters,*
*I want you to always remember that it's normal to struggle,*
*and it's possible to emerge beautiful.*

*Let this be written for a future generation that a*
*people not yet created may praise the Lord.*

— PSALM 102:8

Those who look to Him are radiant.

— PSALM 34:5

# CONTENTS

# PREFACE

Welcome, sweet friend.

I have a tender place in my heart for you. You matter so much to me already. I don't know your name, but I wrote this book for you. The condition of your heart, your soul, and your mindset matters—to me and to God. The things you have lived through, the hurt you have survived, the disappointments you have faced—they're real. I know they are. I get you and God's got you. Thank you for being willing to share your life with me on these pages. I am grateful.

This book is for all of God's girls who feel tired. For women who have been wounded. For women who have been disappointed. For women not sure how to move on or heal up. If life has been a bed of roses and everything has always gone your way, then you won't get much from these pages—other than some comic relief perhaps in knowing that you may not be as crazy as I am.

Read this book with the knowledge that you are loved. You are invited and you are wanted. God sees you and He knows your stuff. I love you. I'll be praying for you.

Amy Joy

1

# GROWING UP, NOT JUST GROWING OLD

*I*'m tired.

I'm not sure when it happened exactly. At some point I started building up a thick wall of self-protection around my heart. Or more like a cement bunker made to withstand weapons of mass destruction. My heart is hardening.

I'm tired of hurt. I'm tired of disappointment. I'm tired of bullies. Some days I'm even tired of people altogether, which seems like an awful thing to say, and makes me feel like a total loser on top of feeling tired. I'm tired of politics, especially in the church. I've run out of patience for cranky Christians. I'm tired of life being hard. I'm tired of feeling like I'm failing. I'm tired of feeling like I'm too much yet clearly not enough. I'm tired of feeling overwhelmed and undernourished. I'm tired of my emotions, my feelings, and my overthinking brain.

I'm tired of being tired.

There's a traffic jam in my soul of people I need to start loving better, but I don't really want to. There are things I need to release, but for the life of me I can't figure out how. Some days I have no idea what exactly to do with my bruised-up, weary soul and my out-of-control mind. I often feel lonely. I often feel like I'm surviving life, doing nothing more than reacting to it as it crashes and unfolds around me.

Because I'm a preacher's wife, sometimes people assume my life is perfect or that I should be. Newsflash: My life isn't perfect and neither am I—not by a long shot. Maybe your life isn't perfect, either. I'd like to hug you right about now.

I struggle to trust people. I read into situations. I assume things that apparently I shouldn't. My husband and I argue about whose perception of an event is actually correct. I tell my man, "I'm not negative, I'm a realist. You're naïve and you just don't have the gift of discernment like I do." (Confession: Most of the time, it's me being negative. *But please don't tell him I just admitted that.*)

I think I think too much.

Oh, bother.

It's exhausting being me some days!

I didn't used to be this way, though. I used to be more kind, outgoing, easygoing, vivacious, positive, joyful, and fun. What happened? Life, I guess? A slow fade and some sloppy living—I guess that's what happened to the person I used to be.

I'm a middle-aged woman with a million blessings. I'm a woman who has all she ever dreamed of. So why on earth do I prefer isolated, bunkered-up living? (Okay—no—actually I'd hate living in an actual bunker. What I'd *really* like is a darling cottage on a private beach with lots of natural light, the sound of waves crashing outside, and last, but certainly not least, my very own personal chef. Sounds great, right?)

I can't be the only, worn out, wiped out, *can-I-please-have-a-time-out*, ready to hide away girl. You have stuff too. We all do. Those women who you think have it all together? Well, they don't. You, my friend, are not alone in your struggle. I'm pouring my little heart out on these pages for you to know that.

I guess you could say that I'm at a crossroads in my life.

Maybe you are too.

———

Over forty years ago, I was a sweet, petite kindergartener in Mrs. Peter's class in Mountain Lake, Minnesota. Growing up in a town with such a lovely name certainly was a delight. However, the name "Mountain Lake" is a bit deceiving. You will find no mountain in Mountain Lake. It's actually more of a mound, really. And while boats populate most other Minnesotan Lakes for endless hours of summer fun, the only thing in this lake is an infestation of weeds. Although it doesn't quite live up to the picturesque image the name evokes, this quaint town of 2,000 people was my home and a wonderful place to spend my childhood days.

It was recess.

Like most days, I was attempting to master my routine on the wooden balance beams, hoping this would be the triumphant day I'd finally conquer all three tiers. My daydreams of being an Olympic gold medalist gymnast hinged on every step. I navigated the beams while waving to the judges and my adoring fans in my imaginary, shiny, sequined leotard.

I attended a very small school. We're talking less than thirty kids in my *entire* grade. Despite the small school size we had a huge, extraordinarily fun playground. This was before the days when fuddy-duddy, paranoid adults made up silly rules in the name of protecting children's safety, ruining all the fun and sucking adventure right out of childhood. Thankfully, I grew up before all *that*.

We had teeter-totters that bruised a few bottoms when "friends" bailed out. The helpless kid at the top dropped back to the ground like a cement block tossed out a second-story window. There was hard cement under the swings instead of soft wood chips and loose rocks under the monkey bars. The climbing towers were way too tall for little kids. A merry-go-round circled at speeds of what seemed like two hundred miles per hour as it launched brave riders all the way across the playground. We had a three-story-high metal slide. Okay, it wasn't actually three stories high, but to this five-year-old it sure seemed like it was. On warmer days, I remember the scorching hot metal peeling the skin off the back of my legs more than once. High speeds and raw flesh . . . I'm cringing at the thought of it now.

But it was *so much fun*. And somehow we all survived.

There I was on that playground, happy of spirit and pure of heart, about to stick the landing of my gold medal-winning Olympic routine, when suddenly, *she* appeared.

I sensed her approaching before I even saw her, and I could tell she wasn't going to be nice. A gigantic second grader stomped right up to me. With clarity and conviction, she rudely knocked me back down to reality as she shouted:

"You're the ugliest girl I have ever seen!"

Then she marched off as arrogant as she came.

My Olympics were over.

My daydreams were dashed.

And my shiny, sequined leotard was no longer so stunning.

*Ugliest. Girl. Ever.*

I graduated with the same handful of kids I started kindergarten with. I saw this same mean girl every day, several times a day, for the next decade of my life. Every time I saw her, I replayed those piercing words in my mind: You're the ugliest girl I have ever seen. I repeated her words over and over and over. I was now labeled forever. The recording wouldn't stop. The label wouldn't come off.

I have a feeling that you've received labels too, in your life. Do any of these sound familiar? Unwanted. Untalented. Failure. Too much. Not enough. Fat. Too skinny. Infertile. Sinful. Abused. Single. Irrational. Stupid. Unlovable. Incapable.

The list goes on and on.

But "Ugliest girl ever?" That one belongs to me. Sorry, folks, but there's only one winner—that'd be me.

I have a theory about these labels and the stories we tell ourselves about them. Remember the tale of the "Ugly Duckling"? I think the story true, but we have it in reverse. That second grader was wrong that day on the playground—I was not *ugly*—but, sometimes, *beautiful* people slowly, unknowingly become *ugly* over time. Not because the mean things bullies say are true, but because we start *believing* that they are. Belief births behavior. Behave a certain way long enough and you will likely make a way of living out of it.

A *beautiful* swan turns into an *ugly* duckling—not the other way around.

As the years wore on, I allowed myself to become *ugly* over time.

And by "ugly," I don't mean "not pretty." I mean bitter, discontent, sad, angry, scared, defeated, empty, insecure, unsure, withdrawn, and lacking in joy or hope. *That* kind of *ugly*. It doesn't take long for the rawness and heartache of life to settle deep into the marrow of your bones. The *ugly* slowly chips away the natural *beauty*. Wearing a cute as can be outfit paired with the perfect pair of darling shoes won't cover it up. A good hair day can't fix it. Not with this kind of *ugly*. (And you and I both know if a good hair day isn't going to help . . . well then, Houston, we have a problem.)

This is what happens when a fifty-year-old woman decided in her twenties and thirties to not do something with the hurt buried deep in her soul. This is what happens when a woman gets a label and she decides to keep it. This is what happens when a woman believes damaging lies about her worth. This is what happens when she never bothers to do the work of stopping the replay and rewriting the script. This is what happens when a woman has handed over her joy to difficult moments one day after another until those days turn into years and those years pile up into decades. Before she even realizes it, *ugly* has set in. Before she even knows how it happened or when it happened she just knows she is *done*. She's empty and tired. This is what I'm afraid is happening to me.

If I do nothing I will continue to grow into *that* kind of *ugly*. I'm certain of it.

In my early twenties I attended a Bible study with some women twice my age. As I listened to those precious older women talk about their issues, I thought to myself: "Wait a minute, that's the stuff I struggle with now! But they're in their forties and fifties? I thought people, like, just, kinda grew up. Don't we mature past this stuff? They've got twenty years on me. What's going on? I thought this would just . . . go away with age . . . ."

I realized right there in our musty church fellowship hall that I wouldn't automatically *grow up*. The only guarantee is growing older. The stuff I struggle with now is the same stuff I will struggle with years from now if I don't decide to *do* something. It won't go away on its own, no matter how much I wish it would.

I can slap on anti-aging cream under my eyes (which I do) or inject Botox into my sagging face (which I don't do), but I will still be the woman who I have developed all these years. I can't spend years believing lies about myself and then expect to become more *beautiful*.

I also spent a great deal of time with elderly women when I was younger working as a nursing assistant. Facing the last years of their lives, these women lived in a place they never wanted to end up: a nursing home. Most of them were bound to wheelchairs and needed help with the most private aspects of personal care. Being completely dependent on others is not an easy way to live. And yet, there were several women I remember who had...

Deep wrinkles, yet a kind face.

Drooping eyelids, yet a loving gaze.

Teeth missing, yet a warm smile.

Weathered skin, yet a soft countenance.

Failing bodies, yet a grateful spirit.

Crooked fingers, yet a comforting touch.

Thinning hair, yet a remarkable confidence.

They had lost their physical vitality yet displayed radiance and contentment. They all experienced the rough stuff of life. Every single one of them pounded the pavement of this planet like you and me are doing right this moment. They didn't get a hall pass on pain. They faced it. They came through it—*well.* Somewhere along the way, these gracious women decided to *grow up* along with growing old. They didn't allow the wounds of life to steal their *beauty.* Their pain didn't embitter them. Their failures didn't stop them. Their bullies didn't beat them. The devil didn't get his way.

I want to be just like those women when I *grow up.* (Maybe with teeth, though . . . I'd really like to keep my own teeth.)

If I want *that,* then I know this (besides the fact that I better start flossing more than once a month): I must deal with my stuff and do business with the Lord. I must let Him heal up my broken heart and bind up my gaping wounds. I must work hard to take control of my thinking. Daily. *Like, I mean it. True beauty* is on the line. I know my future eighty-year-old self is begging me to do that right now before it's too late. I want to be *beautiful* even if I am bound to a wheelchair, even if life has been tough, and even if I don't end up having my own teeth. I want to be gracious and grateful, even still.

Older people can't fake it anymore. Have you noticed that? Who they've actually been all their lives is who you will see in those vulnerable elderly years. The façade falls away. I want *beauty* to be what emerges when I can no longer hide what is going on inside. I will either do a drastic, risky thing with my heart or leave it alone and turn into the very thing that girl called me decades ago: *ugly*. If I don't do this *growing up* thing, all the junk of life will harden my face and heart.

I have a choice. *Grow up* or just *grow old*. *Beautiful* or *ugly*. Which way will I go? There is no neutral road. A road with no destination does not exist. I'm headed somewhere. I will end up somewhere. I will become someone.

*I am at the corner of bitter and sweet.*

————

The chapters of this book are my personal battleground.

They are territory that God and I have fought hard—stinkin' hard—to gain back from the enemy over the last decade. These are the places where God has invited me to *grow up*, battle for *beauty*, and choose *sweet* over *bitter*.

Some seasons He dragged me kicking and screaming. Some seasons I've lagged way behind, sulking in the corner at the pity party I threw for myself. Some seasons I hid from God because I felt unworthy and unwanted, or stubborn and unteachable because I wanted it all to feel fair (but it seldom is). Like the Israelites, I've gone around a few mountains way too many times. It's crazy-stupid, really. Of all His children, God would never claim me as his "easy" one, I can assure you of that.

I've spent a couple of decades ministering to women as both a pastor's wife and a speaker. Here's something that I've observed time and time again, both in myself and others: God invites us, or more like *requires* us, to cooperate in the process of growing up in *beauty* and wholeness. He desires that we flex our spiritual muscles and tap into all that He has already taught us.

There was once a woman in a Bible study I led who told me her husband asked her why she was joining another Bible study since the last one didn't work. My husband could have asked the same of me at times, I'm afraid.

If we want to become the women God knows we are capable

of becoming, He will insist that we use what He has already given us. Did you know that as daughters of the King, we have *all* we need right now in our possession?

> *By his divine power, God has given us everything we need for living a godly life.*

— 2 PETER 1:3

God didn't give us only a couple of things. He gave us *everything* we could possibly stand in need of while we do life here on this big ball called planet earth.

If we're honest, most of us would admit we'd rather God do all the work for us. God is capable of giving us instant, sweat-free, pain-free breakthroughs—of course He is, He is God!—but He usually requires His girls to get off our cute buns to walk with him into godly womanhood. We like instant miracles. But God likes strong daughters even more. We want the road of least resistance, but we also want victory. We can't have both.

If there was an instant and easy road to destination *true beauty*, someone would have found it by now. But not a soul on this planet has. The most beautiful people you could ever meet have walked the darkest roads you could ever imagine. They ended up *beautiful* but, have mercy, I can guarantee you the route to get there wasn't found aboard a luxury cruise ship sailing calm waters. He loves us too much to let life and maturity be easy-peasy for His kids.

Through it all, I see the *beauty* that has emerged from the darkest places of my life. All along the way, God has not given up on me and He will not give up on you.

> *Wisdom brightens a (woman's) face and changes its hard appearance.*

*— ECCLESIASTES 8:1*

*Those who look to Him are radiant.*

*— PSALMS 34:5*

*Being confident of this, that He who began a good work
in you will carry on to completion . . . .*

*— PHILIPPIANS 1:6*

*It is time to break up your unplowed ground for it is
time to seek the Lord until He comes and showers
righteousness on you.*

*— HOSEA 10:12*

God is willing and able to brighten the dark places and shower righteousness upon us. He is. I just know it. But, girl-friend, the deal is you better believe He is going to ask us to engage with Him and do some hard, consistent, and—at times—painful work. Breaking up unplowed ground is no walk in the park. Neither is carrying a good thing on to completion. There's no shortcut to growth or victorious living.

If I want to be radiant, then I need to look to Him. If I'm not willing to break a sweat (mentally, emotionally, *and* spiritually), then I'm not serious about choosing *beauty*. There's no easy three step process. It doesn't happen automatically by the time the dryer buzzes, either. (But only after I washed the same load twice since I forgot the clothes were in the washer so long that the load now stinks to high heaven.) And it won't happen by the time we're done binge watching our favorite TV series while double-dipping tortilla chips in homemade pico de gallo, if that's what floats your boat (it does mine). There will be no easy way. But there *is* a way.

God is telling me, it's *time*.

We're ready whether we think we are or not, you know. If I wait until I'm no longer afraid or tired, or until I finally have the *umption in my gumption*, I will take this *ugly* to the grave. I don't have the luxury of waiting for my feelings to catch up on this one. I will have to start *before* I feel like it. My feelings can book a later flight. Or no flight at all. I'm fine either way.

Whatever it takes, let's commit now to see this *becoming beautiful thing* through. We need courage to face life, don't we? I sure do. We need courage to be brave enough to soften up and let the walls crumble around us. We *will* be hurt again. Pain *will* threaten to drown us again. Our minds *will* attempt to sabotage us again. We will continue to feel depleted and defeated on occasion. None of that will go away as long as we are chugging air.

I wish I could tell you all the hard stuff will stop. I wish I could tell you the danger is gone for good, but we both know that's a bunch of hogwash. We will have to learn how to handle the hard stuff. We will have to come out of hiding *before* we feel safe. The question isn't whether God *can* make a miracle out of us, the question is if we will *let* Him.

*Ugly* isn't worth the walls of self-protection we build up around our wounded hearts. That's far too high of a price for me. I've already seen its impact on me and I don't like it. Not one little bit.

As we close this chapter and begin this journey together, I want to tell you what I've found to be the most reliable, fail-proof *beauty* treatment available to us today (Bonus: It's free!): a current heart with God. Keep one. Apply daily.

If a woman is going to kick *ugly* to the curb she needs a heart that knows her God well. She spends time, logs miles, and shares memories with Him. She treasures her Bible. She feeds her soul. She praises more than she pouts. She speaks the Word of God throughout her day. She worships Him freely and frequently. She is more grateful than she is grumpy. She spends her time wisely. She lives with an unapologetic confidence because she is, after all, loved by her Abba Father. She knows that's all she needs to walk securely in this world.

Let me remind you, dear one, in case life has dulled your awareness of the truth, you're a beloved daughter of the King of Kings. He delights over you with singing. He rejoices at the sight of you. You're the apple of His eye. He is crazy about you. He thinks about you. He likes you. A lot. He does. God likes you! We will chat more about this in our final chapter together. I can't wait.

For now, I need you to know that no matter who (even if that "who" is *you*) has told you otherwise, you're, without a doubt, 100% loved, 100% accepted and 100% wanted. Yes, *you are!* Take my word for it, borrow my faith for a while if you have to. That's fine. I have done the same from others from time to time. But promise me you will start *here*. Ask God to help you begin to live from a place of being completely loved, from the top of your precious head to the tips of your cute toes. Because you are. I've had to learn the hard way that if I don't get *this*, I don't stand a chance in this fight for *beautiful* living.

Girls, *ugly* is easy. *Beauty* is not. But I want *beauty*. I think you do too. We really can *grow up* while growing old. *Beauty* can abound right alongside of our ever increasing wrinkles. Forget the Botox and coconut oil, ladies. We have something better.

I'm ready. It's time.

*Hey there, feelings. I'll see you on the other side.*

I'm excited to take this journey together—you, me, and our Jesus. It'll be a really good ride because He is along for it.

---

## CHOOSING SWEETNESS: GOING DEEPER WITH GOD

*May the beauty of the Lord be upon us.*

— PSALMS 90:17

*Create in me a pure heart, O God, and renew a right spirit within me.*

— PSALMS 51:10

- What lies have you believed about yourself? What labels have you replayed over and over in your head?
- Do you sense your heart hardening? What has made you tired? Describe how you feel about yourself and your life right now.
- In what areas have you truly *grown up*? Celebrate your journey. Thank God for the ways you are exhibiting *beauty* and becoming like those radiant older women.
- Are there ways you know God is asking you to get involved in your personal journey to victory and health?
- Do you live loved? If you began to live loved, how would that change how you behave?
- Talk to God about what you're processing.

———

## SWEET NUGGETS: TAKEAWAYS TO REMEMBER

*Belief births behavior.*

13

*I have a choice: Grow up or grow old.*

*A road with no destination or no consequences doesn't exist. I will end up somewhere. I will become someone.*

*God loves me too much to let life and maturity be easy-peasy.*

*If I'm going to kick ugly to the curb, I need a heart that knows my God well.*

*Living loved is necessary if I want to experience victorious living.*

*The question isn't if God is able to make a miracle out of me, the question is will I let Him.*

*God didn't give me only a couple of things, He gives me everything I could possibly need.*

## 2

## HE DID NOT GIVE ME WHAT I WANTED

*T*he darling two story Yellow House on the dead end street was going to be home.

*Our* home.

I was certain of it and I couldn't stop dreaming about it.

I had the paint selected, the walls decorated, and the furniture arranged before we even made so much as an offer. (I tend to go a little overboard—I do realize that.) I plain fell in love at first sight.

On the wraparound porch, I imagined greeting the morning sunshine with Jesus, a fabulous cup of *fu-fu* coffee in hand. You know, that's a little bit of coffee with a lot of cream and sugar. (The house didn't actually have a porch—yet. But we would add one—someday. Make that *only-in-my-dreams* kind of someday.) I visualized a studio apartment on top of the garage for our out-of-state parents. (Alright, make that the *only-in-my-dreams* kind of someday too. Sigh.)

You could call me a tad presumptuous, but I'd call it a longing to make a home.

There were so many things about the house that were

perfect for us. For example, the backyard touched school campus property for elementary through high school. A playground that we didn't have to buy or attempt to assemble, property we didn't have to pay taxes on, and a lawn we didn't have to mow: That was all I needed to convince my man. And we are talking *walking* to school! No carpooling. No lines. No traffic. Send the kids out the back door two minutes before the school bell rings. That's it! My mornings would be a glorious mommy-style piece of coffee cake. My kids would come bounding through the back door after school. I wouldn't even need to glance at the clock once the entire day. (I always feared forgetting what time it was and being *that* mom who leaves her kids waiting like helpless orphans at the curb.)

There was the bike path which led to hundreds of miles of bike trails a few blocks down the street. A hop, skip, and jump away was historic Main Street with its quaint shops, Dairy Queen, movie theater, coffee shops, library, post office, river views, a restaurant called the Dam Bistro (I was looking forward to saying its name out loud in front of my sorta over-saved husband, Cory. "Oversaved" isn't a word. I made up the term for my highly conservative, nearly perfect man. Once you get to know him you'll understand.)

And . . . did I mention the Dairy Queen? (Okay, so maybe the Dairy Queen was more like a hop, skip, and jump down a *very* steep seven-block-long hill, but never mind that. I needed the exercise.)

Oh, and a white picket fence around my darling Yellow House was in the plans too. You didn't think I'd forget the white picket fence, did you?

It was the realistic, affordable, and in-our-budget kind of perfect. It did need work. A ton of work. It was an ordinary house that had its issues for sure. My husband and I aren't the "handy" types, per se. But with a little TLC, a whole lot of

16

Pinterest inspiration, and some serious DIY YouTube-watching, we'd figure it out. Right?

This would be life for our little family. It worked for our teeny tiny, barely-making-ends-meet-we-qualify-for-reduced-school-lunches kind of budget. It was perfect for us.

At that time, a church parsonage was what we had been calling home for the past seven years. It wasn't that we didn't like the parsonage, we did. It was more of a house than we could have afforded in that area. Bigger than The Yellow House, for sure. There was a gorgeous 1,330-acre state park out the back door. The back door! We hiked in that park nearly every day. We loved where we lived.

But . . . how shall I say this? The house had been neglected for many years. I once overheard an elder saying: "It'd take $20,000 to make this house livable."

But we *were* living in it.

There was mold in the partially finished basement. Sewer water and sink disposal remains regurgitated through the laundry room drain on to our floor. The house was a wood-pecker haven covered in rotted siding. (There is nothing like trying to get three kids to take naps while a woodpecker slams his head into the side of the house.) Fake wood paneling adorned nearly every wall and paper thin green carpet made it feel like a game of perpetual mini-golf. *Cool.*

Last but not least, the mice ate food right out of our cupboards. Seems they took fondly to our home too.

A woman from church stopped by one summer afternoon as I was painting the shutters because . . . how do I put this politely? That hunter green hue was just not working for me.

The woman told me I shouldn't paint the shutters because the next pastor's wife might not like the color I choose. I told her the next pastor's wife could paint the shutters whatever color her sweet little heart desired. (I did say it with a humorous tone, in case you were wondering.) We did have permission from the church board to make painting decisions on our own —in case you were wondering that too.

When the Yellow House came on the market we decided: Let's buy this place and move out of the parsonage, and let's stay in the Yellow House forever. Let's make this quaint little town on the Wisconsin-Minnesota scenic byway home for the long haul. There was something about committing to one community and one church that sounded wonderfully welcome to this heart of mine. I longed to watch our kids grow up while growing old with my husband in one place. Did we dare dream that it's possible that God would actually let us? Could we, please? Let us, as a pastor's family, have what most people think is normal? A place and community to call home, for good, and a place to belong for as long as we desired, even forever. I wanted to plant roots down deep. *Pretty please.*

I wanted to do motherhood with my friends while our kids also became friends. I wanted to see my friends' kids grow up. I wanted them to see mine grow up. I wanted to have conversations about my adult kids with people who actually *knew* my kids.

Tell me there's a woman out there who understands.

So we waited. Not from a call from the realtor or the bank. We waited for a call from the church elders. The decision wasn't ours to make. They got to vote, we did not. Church boards consist of volunteers, which means seldom do things get accomplished urgently. When you're waiting to buy a foreclosed home, as we were, one thing you don't have is the luxury of time. Our urgency wasn't their emergency and the issue was tabled for next month's agenda.

Upon returning home after being out of town for a few days, I begged my ever patient husband to swing by *our* Yellow House.

SOLD.

My daydreams had become someone else's dream come true. Later that evening, we found out that a family from our church had purchased it. I tried to be happy for them. But I wasn't. I really thought God was going to give it to us.

The following day an elder pulled into our driveway, oblivious to what had transpired. Like he was just dropping off his dry cleaning or running any other unimportant errand, he casually informed us: *We wanted to let you know the Elder Board decided that you cannot buy your own home.*

I can't remember the words my husband uttered but I'm certain they were kind, mature, and gracious. He always is. (And sometimes that makes me mad. Is that odd? I mean seriously, I just want him to get mad about something someday.)

On the outside I faked it really well. But on the inside, my guts were a mess.

I was mad that a group of volunteers from my husband's workplace could dictate our private lives and take so long in doing so. My disappointment turned to hurt and anger. I wanted our private lives and personal finances to be private and personal. We should be able to make decisions on our own with our family and our future in mind. Fish bowl-living in a parsonage smack dab next to my husband's workplace where his boss and secretary could watch all our comings and goings was getting *really* old. And we were only in our twenties. I was either going to *grow up* or *grow old* right then and there. *Beauty* was on the line again and *ugly* was coming for me.

I was mad at God but I blamed man. It's easier that way. Blaming man instead of believing God sounded good to my broken heart. Besides, my frustration needed a target I could see.

We do this a lot, don't we? I know I do. It's easier to blame the president, the teacher, or the boss than it is to trust that God has something bigger going on. For example, maybe the coach benched your kid because God wants your kid benched. Maybe God is working on increasing your child's depth of character. Maybe there are great life lessons God wants developed in your child's heart and mind to prepare him for his life assignment. Maybe your child will be a coach one day himself or a therapist or a parent. Maybe developing the Fruits of the Spirit in your child is more important to God than developing their stat sheet. Will we believe God or blame man?

If I trusted God I'd have to release my dreams and admit it wasn't God's best for us. I wasn't ready to do that. So I vented. Not to people, mind you. Church unity, not to mention my husband's job, was on the line and that mattered more to me. It has always been hard for me that my husband's job depends on my actions. But not as hard as it's on him I'm sure. (Sorry, honey. I do add spunk to your life, right? You're welcome.)

So instead, I vented to the woman looking back at me in the mirror.

*Ugly* and I were eyeballing each other.

I wasted a great deal of time ruminating and fuming. I had ridiculous make believe conversations in my head. Boy, did it ever feel good in the moment. But what I was doing was toxic to my soul, demoralizing to my spirit, and devastating my heart. I didn't get what I wanted. I pouted. *Welcome to life, Amy. You're not winning any awards for maturity, by the way.*

About a year later, God called our family away from that community and from the church family we loved. God saw what we couldn't: He was going to move us away. That's why He didn't let us buy The Yellow House. He cared very much about our family's future and our finances. What I thought the Elders ruined, God was protecting us from all along. I didn't see that coming. Sorry, God, for having a royal fit over something you had figured out. You're pretty good at this sovereign-ruling-of-the-Universe thing.

I wouldn't plant roots, I wouldn't raise my kids with the women I started motherhood with, they wouldn't see my kids grow up, and I wouldn't see theirs grow up either. We wouldn't do life together for the long haul after all. I'm wiping tears as I type. Why is this so emotional for me? It shouldn't be such a big deal to my soul, but it just is. We were made for community. We were made for relationship. We were made to know and be known. Losing all of that requires grieving. That's precisely why it's so hard.

God sent us out of the place we longed to be forever and to a state where we didn't know a soul and no one knew us. We had no history, no memories, no shared life with the new people God called us to. We yanked our roots up and started completely over.

I'm not good at moving. Frankly, I think I'm allergic to it. If that's not a real thing, it should be. I grew up in one community and my parents still live there, in the same house I was raised in. They attend the same church with the same people who changed my diapers in the nursery. I feel like that's how life should go. Uprooting is unsettling to this heart of mine that loves depth of relationships and tradition.

When it seems like the plans I have for my life are not falling into place, I try to remember The Yellow House and—deep breath here—*trust God*. He reserves the right to use unfair circumstances to do His good, pleasing, and perfect will—in our lives and in our children's lives too. God does not hesitate to direct our steps and grow us into maturity while simultaneously revealing the crud in our hearts. He will go for greater mileage out of a trial every time. He logged some miles on me over The Yellow House for sure. Killed two birds with that stone. God is a good shot.

I've had to learn that it's best if I don't expect God's will for my life to unfold painlessly. God isn't afraid of pain and he doesn't have an issue with asking us to do hard things. Doesn't seem to faze Him in the least.

His path for my life and yours may come about in ways we perceive as unfair. God will use any means necessary to grow us into His likeness and keep us in His perfect will. *Any means.* Unfair means, ugly means, maddening means, hurtful means, disappointing means. There isn't a thing God won't use for good. Stubborn bosses, unfair coaches, insensitive teachers, irritating co-workers, demanding neighbors. You name it, He can use it. See Him and believe Him. Don't blame *them.* You will emerge more *beautiful* if you do. So will your kiddos.

———

I'm delighted to report that we own our own home now. (Well, the bank owns it, but they don't care a hill of beans what color I paint my shutters.) It's gray with black shutters and a red front door. It has a darling porch that came with the house. (Turns out I didn't need to wait for a *someday.*) I enjoy my cup of coffee and my Jesus on that porch pretty much every day. We have a sunroom, an acre sized lot, a lilac bush (my favorite flower), and several perennial gardens. It all brings me such joy.

This house isn't right next to the school, but we have many precious memories of singing, talking, and blessing our kids each groggy morning in our faithful, dented up family van. Waiting (not always so patiently) in line to pick up my kids after school proved to be a powerful time of prayer. Only once (maybe twice) was I *that* mother who forgot to pick up her kids. But they survived. And I wasn't reported for child neglect. *Thank you, Jesus.*

There is no state park down the street. But there's a lovely park a mile away with a disc golf course which my husband and son love. A fantastic community swimming pool has saved the day on many a scorching summer afternoon. A cheap ice cream shop is within biking distance. My husband has a perfectly paved country road on which he enjoys his coveted long bike rides. And our house is situated just on the edge of town which means I can enjoy walks around the country block.

As it turns out, this home is perfect for us. It's more than I could have asked or imagined or dared to dream. God went way beyond with this one. It was a personal gift from Him. I know it was. He knew my heartache in losing The Yellow House and having to uproot our family and say those heartbreaking good-byes to a church family we were crazy about. He was kind enough to bless us more abundantly than our previous dreams ever could have. It doesn't always turn out this way. Many times it doesn't. But *this* time it did.

Life in our current community is completely different from what it would have been in our last. There are days when I wonder what life would have been like right now had we gotten to stay. I'll never know. I miss our friends very much. I hope they miss me too. Those dreams had to die so we could live new ones. These are the ones God had planned for us as we fulfill his purposes for our lives and our kingdom assignment on this earth.

Living in one home, in one community, attending one church for a lifetime—that's what I thought I wanted. It's what I thought I *needed*. It's what I thought God was going to bless us with. But I'm thankful God doesn't always let me have what I think I want. I look back on my life and recognize many occasions when I wanted something but God didn't give it to me. He had something different in mind. The different thing wasn't always *better*, but it has always been *good*. A God kind of good. With a deep breath of trust, God's idea of good has become good with me.

As I look back on The Yellow House, I see that it wasn't the elders' fault after all; they didn't cost us our dream. *God did.* God intervened. God used the elder board to accomplish His will. The elders were never to blame nor did they deserve my criticism. They had a decision to make with a church budget in mind. It wasn't personal. But God certainly was.

I wrote these words a few months after we moved as I was grieving the loss of leaving our life and embracing the new one:

*Be grateful for what was.* For the good moments you had. Remember those times with a smile on your face. It was good. Celebrate what *was*.

*Accept what is.* This is your new reality. It's not where you thought you would be. It's not what you thought you wanted. But it's your reality nonetheless. It's best if you can learn to accept that. You'll miss what you had and grieve what you didn't get for awhile. That's okay. But spending too much time dwelling on *that* will rob you of *this* day and rob those you love of *you*. It's hard to be present while mentally stuck in the past. Those days in the past no longer exist, but you do.

*Anticipate what is to come.* There are good days ahead. Stay excited for your future and for the great things God has in store for you still. You'll get through this time of grieving and transition. You will. Anticipate life beyond this and keep piling up the days. Blessings are ahead.

You may be grieving the loss of a man you were sure you were going to marry, a job you thought you would be offered, a friendship you believed was deeper than the issue that ended it, a goal you believed you would achieve, the possession you were desperate for . . . . There are so many things that we thought, for sure, God would give us but he didn't. With a great deal of tenderness, can I encourage you to take a deep breath of trust and resist the urge to blame?

———

I live in The Gray House now. I love it. A lot.

My dream is to live here forever.

But I want His dreams for my life even more.

I hear His voice every now and then whispering to me: "Amy, believe me and trust me when I don't give you what you think you want. Sweetie, someday I promise, you will thank me for not letting you have it."

———

**Choosing Sweetness: Going Deeper with God**

*He works all things together for good to those who love Him and are called according to His purpose.*

— ROMANS 8:28

*I know, O Lord, that a man's life isn't his own, it is not for man to direct his steps.*

— JEREMIAH 10:23

*Many are the plans of a man's heart, but it's the Lord's purposes that prevail.*

— PROVERBS 19:21

*Trust in the Lord with all of your heart, lean not on your own understanding, in all of your ways acknowledge Him and He will direct your path.*

— PROVERBS 3:5-6

- What are the things, both big and small, that you wanted but didn't receive? Things that you were certain God would give you. Are you blaming man or believing God through that disappointment?
- Do you believe that God sees what you can't and knows what you don't and therefore you can rest in His sovereignty over your life?
- Is there anything in your life that you can now see in hindsight and say, "Thank you, God, for not giving me what I thought I wanted." It could be a man, a job, a possession, a home . . . . Can you see that God was either protecting you or preparing you for something else?
- Think of ways in which you're grateful for what was, accepting of what is, and anticipating what is to come. Tell Jesus how you feel about each of these things. Be honest with yourself and with Him.

---

## SWEET NUGGETS: TAKEAWAYS TO REMEMBER

*Do not have a royal fit over something God has figured out.*

*Believe God instead of blaming man.*

*I won't expect God's will for my life to unfold painlessly.*

*God isn't afraid to ask me to do hard things.*

*I will trust God when He doesn't give me what I think I want. Someday I will thank Him for not letting me have it.*

*God sees what I cannot. He knows what I do not know.*
*Take a deep breath and trust Him.*

# 3

# THIS TIME I WILL PRAISE

*T*he senior pastor we worked for during my husband's college internship was having an affair.

I was his new secretary and I knew he was having an affair on my first day on the job. It was obvious. I couldn't believe it wasn't obvious to the rest of the world.

Have you ever wondered why everyone else on this civilized planet doesn't see what you're seeing? I wasn't sure if I was a complete nutcase or if I was the only one *not* nuts.

I decided to say something. I thought I was going to save the church from unthinkable disaster. And I thought I'd save both couples' marriages too. I was doing the right thing, the wise thing, the biblical thing, the thing anyone in my shoes would do . . . right?

Wrong.

The pastor denied the accusation. He had the power and charisma to charm his way out of anything. Also, this was twenty-five years ago and he knew there wasn't a thing a little female intern like me could do about it anyway. He had the entire church leadership and congregation fooled. And he then proceeded to rub my face in their affair every day. He was rude and inappropriate to me in countless ways. He forced me to cover for him and even lie to his wife. He punished me for speaking the truth. It was a tremendous burden on my young soul.

I should have quit my job right then and there but my husband needed to graduate. His diploma was riding on this experience going well. So I shut my mouth and did my job. (Not very well though, mind you. Not only did I have trouble working for the man because of the situation, I also had trouble transferring phone calls. *Oops.* Clip art in the bulletins, however? I nailed that.)

Before this, I had no idea that a pastor could do this sort of thing and still get up before his people to preach on a Sunday morning. How could a man of God live a lie in front of his congregation? I figured he should have flat out fainted on stage, or at least upchucked the Cheerios he ate for breakfast. He did neither. I grew up in a Christian bubble and then at the ripe old age of twenty-one, discovered that a pastor could be a con artist. I was in turmoil over the whole filthy mess of it. It made me question everything I believed about church, male authority, leadership, and trust.

A full three years later, the truth finally came out to the rest of the congregation. The church hired a team of professional mediators to help clean up the mess, but from my perspective, the clean-up process was as dysfunctional as the affair itself.

All the church members sat there while the lead mediator told us to—*get this*—just *believe* that the affair never happened. He declared that, under the blood of Jesus, that the affair should now be forgotten. It never existed and that we were prohibited from speaking about it or asking any questions. And I sat in the back of the sanctuary weeping.

We weren't allowed to be broken. We weren't allowed to

grieve or process or ask God for cleansing and forgiveness. We weren't allowed to mourn or to feel. We didn't repent as a body. We were commanded to simply believe it didn't happen.

But it did.

I expected so much more. I expected wrongs to be made right. I expected light to burst through the darkness. I expected health to emerge from the toxicity. I expected closure. I expected cleansing. I expected biblical repentance. I expected permission to process. I expected transparency. I expected those in authority to make wise decisions. I expected men to be manly. I expected leaders to lead. I expected them to do hard things. I expected hired professionals to know what they were doing. I expected God to fix what was broken. I expected God to make me feel better. I expected so much more.

In the years since then, I have found some comfort in a story about a woman named Leah. Leah understood this desperate desire for something to fix what should never have happened in the first place. She, like many women in scripture, lived through a R-rated nightmare—one I can't even begin to fathom. One that makes my little heartache look like a lovely walk in the park on a sunny day at a perfect seventy-three degrees.

Leah's real life story is grueling. If you're not familiar with it, you can read it in Genesis 29. The gist of it's that Leah's younger sister, Rachel, was engaged to be married to a man who had been pursuing her. His name was Jacob. He loved Rachel. Their relationship is one of the only true romances we get a glimpse of in the Bible.

But there was a problem.

The custom in those days was for a father to give his eldest daughter in marriage first before the youngest. Leah was less attractive than her little sister Rachel. Rachel was beautiful. The father of the two girls concluded that the only way a man would marry his elder, less attractive daughter would be to trick a man into doing so. If his youngest daughter married before his oldest then the unwanted one would be alone and labeled for the rest of her life.

The father came up with a plan. He tricked his future son-in-law, Jacob, by switching his daughters at the altar. (Nothing like adding a little family drama into a wedding day!) Jacob ends up marrying—are you ready for this—his bride-to-be's sister. And you thought *your* family had issues. Perhaps we are not as dysfunctional as we thought we were. You're welcome.

Do you wonder where Rachel was on her wedding day? We don't hear a peep from her in this part of the story. Did her father lock her up in the attic like Cinderella? Was she gagged? *Like, seriously, where was the Bride?* She was either hauled off, silenced somehow, or she went along with it. Maybe out of love for her sister she decided to go along with it. Maybe she was fearful of her father so she had no choice but to cooperate. We don't know. I keep thinking Rachel will come bounding down the aisle at any moment, flinging her arms like a crazy woman, sporting serious raccoon eyes and messy hair screaming, "Stop! Wait, I object! That's my man! That's my dress! That's my ring! This is my wedding day! Back off, sis!"

I have a lot of questions about this story in the Bible, actually. This is a great time for me to tell you that I think herein lies the reason that God ordained men to pen the scriptures. We all know there's no woman this side of heaven who could have recorded these stories without the important details. We want to know what people were thinking and feeling. We want the *whole* story. Women would have asked God endless questions. We would've delayed the writing process and driven God nutty. He knew: Men won't ask questions or beg me for more details than I have time and space to give. (That's my take on it, anyway!)

Back to the story. Jacob, the groom, woke up the next

morning in bed with Leah who he thought would be his sister-in-law, but who was now his wife. He was expecting Rachel to be his wife but she was now his sister-in-law.

Are you still with me? I told you it's an R-rated mess. Interestingly, Jacob is upset with his father in law for deceiving him, yet that's precisely what Jacob himself did years' prior—he deceived his own father by stealing the birthright that belonged to his older brother. Remember that from Genesis 27? Jacob got a taste of his own medicine, you could say.

Jacob: "What on earth? Why are you in bed with me? Where is my wife Rachel? I don't want you. Did we...?"

If you're wondering how on earth that could happen, here's how: a heavy veil and some heavy booze.

Poor Leah. There would be no happily ever after for her.

But leave it to God. He sees that Leah is unloved. He cares that she feels completely broken. Leah mattered to God. So God does what God does so well: He shows Leah love by blessing her in another area of her life. He gives her children.

*When the Lord saw that Leah was not loved, he opened her womb, but Rachel was barren.*

— GENESIS 29:31

Likely for the first time ever in her life, Leah had something Rachel did not. She would end up becoming the mom to seven precious little boys.

Yet these gifts God gave her actually brought Leah disappointment. She expected the gifts to give her something they were never meant to give. She wanted the gifts from God to fix her heartache. She wanted her kids to make her husband love her.

Leah became pregnant and gave birth to a son. She named

him Reuben and said, "It's because the Lord has seen my misery. Surely my husband will love me now." She conceived again and when she gave birth to a son she said, "Because the Lord heard that I'm not loved he gave me this one too." Again she gave birth to another son and she said, "Now at last my husband will become attached to me because I have borne him three sons." (Genesis 29: 32-43)

You already know what Leah did not. Kids won't fix a dysfunctional marriage. They'll make you tired. Exhaustion, along with a heaping of the greatest of delights and deepest of joys, that's what they'll give you. They are not a remedy for a messed up marriage.

Still, Leah hoped.

She cried out, "Surely my husband will love me now." But he never did. "Now at last my husband will become attached to me . . . ." But he never was.

Instead of seeing how God loved her and was good to her in the midst of her pain, she wanted more. Instead of receiving her sons as the precious gifts they were, she wanted her children to be a cure-all. She wanted the gifts God gave her to do *more* for her. She expected wrongs to be made right. She expected closure on her pain. She expected to feel better about her marriage. God gave Leah a gift, but Leah wanted more.

Sound familiar?

I believe that God was trying to communicate something like this to her:

"I see you, Leah. I know your struggle, I know you were wronged, I know you were rejected, and I know you'll never get a happily ever after with a husband who deeply loves you. But I love you. I will bless your life immensely in other ways. Stop looking for something to fix everything and start looking at what blessings you have already."

Can we receive God's gifts of love without further expectations? Or are we only thankful when we get what we want out of them?

For example, imagine that your elementary-aged daughter is lonely. She is sad and lacks friendships at school. One day she receives an invite to a birthday party.

We start sounding like Leah: "*Surely now*, my daughter will have friends, the girls will accept her, she won't be sad at school. *Now at last* they will include her at recess, they will sit with her at lunch. She'll be popular and surely be the homecoming queen. Wait—she's only in third grade. But still, this is her moment! She'll be happy. And if she's happy that means I'll be happy too. *Surely* if I'm happy, I'll stop eating so many Oreos and lose those ten pounds. If I lose weight, *now at last* I'll fit into my skinny jeans—the ones I threw on the top shelf because they don't fit. Thank you, Lord, for the birthday party invitation!"

Then, on Monday after said birthday party rolls around, those same girls make your daughter cry. Just like they did before the party.

So much for the homecoming queen and skinny jeans. Bummer.

We are disappointed that we didn't get what we wanted from God's gifts to us. We were after *more*. The "surely nows" and "now at lasts" didn't come. We hoped *this* would do it, fix it, change it—but it fell short. God was kind enough to show us love but that love didn't produce what we expected. So we end up hurt when God was simply showing us love in the midst of the tough stuff we were facing.

The deal is, we often want the gifts of God to fix issues they were never intended to fix. We assume that's his primary job: fixing things. It's not.

No one can undo what my rebellious pastor did twenty-five years ago. That pastor chose to take advantage of a vulnerable woman. He groomed her and used his power, authority, and position to get what he wanted. Thankfully, we now live in a different time. As women we feel power now to stand up for ourselves and get out of abusive, demeaning situations. I wouldn't work for a man like that today.

But the problem is, I expected God to fix what happened when the truth came out. Nothing was fixed. I wanted closure. That never came. I wanted the pastor to pay for what he did. He didn't have to do that, either. (Or at least within our church, he didn't. He may have faced other consequences later that I'm unaware of.)

No one could fix what happened to Leah. Her dad couldn't take back what he had orchestrated even if he wanted to. Jacob couldn't force himself to love her. Rachel couldn't trade places with her sister or become less attractive so Leah would feel better.

No one could fix it. It was what it was.

Do you have things in your life like that? I know I sure do.

For example, in my own marriage.

My husband is kind and attentive to me. He truly is an amazing man and husband.

But he is not a protector like I long for him to be, like I spent years expecting him to be. I want him to fight for me and defend me. But it isn't in his disposition or his personality to do so. My heart hurt so much over it. If someone wounds me, he'll tell me to turn the other cheek. ("Oversaved," remember?)

I spent a couple of decades longing for my man to get mad. He never did, and he likely never will. I want him to think poorly of people who hurt me (for like five minutes, is all) or at least be offended on my behalf. He sees the best and believes the best about *everyone*, including people who crush me. I have felt like checking into the loony bin over it.

And from his end, my husband spent years wishing I was a tad less spunky, a whole lot less discerning, and a smidgen less opinionated. I can wear my man right out. Let's just say I have

no problem putting words to my feelings, ideas and beliefs—
hence, this book!

I do have the capacity and soundness of mind to realize that
so much is still so right in my life even though I have areas that
feel wrong. I have wasted far too much time obsessing over the
hard places in my life, which means I don't have the mental
space to see all the blessings. I kept hoping this time things will
change. *Surely now* I will get what I need and *then* I'll feel better.
But nothing has changed and I don't feel better about any of it.
By being so consumed with what is wrong I've missed out on
enjoying the blessings I already have. God has shown me
incredible love by giving me a husband who is good to me in
countless ways. So what exactly am I whining about, right?

I need to spend more time in the next twenty-five years of
our marriage thanking God for the blessing of who my man is
and not complaining about who he is not.

You may long for acceptance from a parent or someone you
admire. You may ache for something you're not getting from
your boyfriend or husband. You may have been violated,
rejected, or betrayed. You may have a messed up relationship
with a family member. Hard places take up a great deal of our
time, mental real estate, and energy, don't they?

I want nothing more than for you to be done with it. *Just
plain done.* By all means, keep praying. Keep asking God for a
miracle and a breakthrough, for restoration and a new beginning. Absolutely. Believe God to do a big thing in your impossible thing. I'm just saying—be done obsessing. Be done
overthinking it. Be done dwelling on it. Be done talking it to
death. Be done expecting something to fix it and being upset
that nothing is. Stop hinging your joy on it.

Give it to the only One who is capable of working the thing
out for good. If you start doing that, I promise you will begin to
be freed up to enjoy your day to day life as it unfolds and you

will be able to see all that's so good and right in your life. You'll start seeing the good in the people around you too.

This is where we *grow up* instead of growing old. This is where *beauty* wins out. Right here, in this tough-as-nails place where we decide to be done with our desperate attempt to change what we have no power to change.

———

After Leah's fourth son is born, she finally learns the lesson and simply says:

*"This time, I will praise."*

I love that. This time, I will see the gift for what is and praise God for it. I will thank the Lord for this blessing right smack in the midst of the unfairness of my life. I stop defining my life by my lack and start defining it by your love.

Thank you, Jesus. Period.

When I accept my reality, my life as it is and my past as it was, I grow *beautiful*. I become radiant. Gracious. Kind. Joyful. Peaceful. Loving. Restful.

Leah never had a loving marriage but she did get the incredible joy of being a mom. God showed her love and blessed her socks off in *other* ways. He has done the same for us. You have messed up places, sure, but you also have over the top blessings in other places!

*This time, I will praise.*

Praising God is such a powerful mood changer. There was a time that my prayer life needed a detox so I decided for a whole month to only give praise. The rule was that I could only thank, worship, and praise him. No begging, no pleading, no requests. I'd be with Him, in His presence in a posture of praise.

It did wonders to reboot my prayer life and get me off my whiny, "gimme-gimme" attitude before the King of the

Universe. In fact, I may need to consider doing that again real soon.

Do you think that God sometimes just wants us to *be* with Him? To sit on His lap. To be His little girl. I bet it thrills His heart when we enter His presence just because we want to be near Him, not because we have a request. Imagine a father with a three year-old. He enjoys his little girl approaching him and yanking on his hand to play or asking to read a book or do something for her. But there is a whole other level of delight when that same little girl crawls up in her daddy's lap just to sit contentedly. Not needing a single thing. Just wanting to be close to her dad. That's all.

What if on occasion we came to our King already full, satisfied, content and ready to bless Him. If I believe He is enough why don't I act like it when I approach His throne? There will always be needs and concerns and requests. Always. Can I put those aside for a moment every now and then, crawl up in His lap just because I think he is the coolest father ever? Being together makes us both happy.

My husband and I were talking with a man in our church when his severely autistic son interrupted us. He wrapped his arms tight around his daddy's legs, declaring (in a little too loud of a voice, but no one minded): "This is my daddy! I love him!"

Aww.

Have you told God lately that you cannot get enough of Him? That you love Him and you are super-duper glad he is your daddy? Do you squeeze Him tight around His neck because you cannot help yourself?

I remember as a little girl standing at our dining room picture window. I waited and watched for my daddy to come home from work. I could spot him walking down the sidewalk about a block away. I was so excited as I caught the first glimpse of him. I would watch him the entire way and then run to him as he came through the door. I didn't need anything from him, I just wanted *him*. I would sit on his shoe with my legs and arms wrapped tight around his leg. He would walk around with me attached to him. I didn't want to let go. My daddy was home and all was well in my little girl soul.

As I look back on the last two decades of my life, one of my greatest regrets has been this fixation on the things that went wrong and are wrong. Friends, the wrongs you have endured are real. They are hard. If you're struggling with not having closure over a wrong you have endured please know that you're not alone in this battle. I want you to have the thing that took me far too long to receive: freedom from it.

God invites us to free ourselves from the expectations of wrongs being made right so we can finally see that God is blessing us preciously and abundantly in other places of our life. This time, praise Him. This time, focus on the sweet loving relationship you and God share.

You know, Leah was never going to get the feeling she was after. She wouldn't have the luxury of a happily ever after with a man. She could either spend her whole life on a desperate attempt to get what she craved or stop expecting it and start seeing all she already had. The miracle God was offering Leah would not be found in Jacob finally loving her. The miracle God was offering Leah was even better; it was for her to live loved regardless.

This time, I will praise.

———

CHOOSING SWEETNESS: GOING DEEPER WITH GOD

*How good it is to sing praises to our God, how pleasant
and fitting to praise Him!*

— PSALM 147:1

*Those who seek the Lord lack no good thing.*

— PSALM 34:10

*Bless the Lord, O my soul, and forget not all His benefits.*

— PSALM 103:2

- Are there any wrongs in your life that you fear will never be made right? How are you processing that?
- Are you obsessing over anything from your past or currently feeling desperate to have something fix those situations?
- Can you see God's love and blessings in your life in other areas?
- Apart from someone or something changing, what miracle is God offering *you*?

———

SWEET NUGGETS: TAKEAWAYS TO REMEMBER

*Attaching expectations to a blessing often leads to discouragement.*

*The gifts God gives me do not need to do more for me.*

*God is blessing my life in other ways.*

*Accept what happened and then get on with living.*

*So much is so right even when so much is so wrong.*

*Define life by God's love, not by my lack.*

*We all have messed up places, but we also have blessed places.*

*Get to God simply to be near Him, not to get something from Him.*

*God is offering a miracle in the midst of the mess.*

# 4

## SO I SAY TO MYSELF

*I* have a secret to tell you. Several years ago I went on a little shopping spree . . . *with tithe money.*

Hold on, now. Before you shut your front door and call your BFF over this one, no, I didn't *steal* tithe money from the offering plate.

Not exactly. Well, sort of.

This was our tithe money that we were going to put in the offering plate that Sunday.

Up until that point I had never spent more than $50 without dialoguing with my man about it. Never. We do the envelopes. If you do too, then you know what I'm talking about. If you don't have the slightest clue what I'm referring to, consider yourself blessed and don't ask too many questions. Ignorance is bliss on this one. (And by the way, Dave Ramsey, thank you for the prison—ummm—I mean freedom found within your nifty envelopes. My husband loves you. Me? Well, you're growing on me, at least, after all these years. I will give you that much.)

I spent about $500 and I loved every minute of it. I bought a lamp that didn't come in a box. You know, the kind in a box with three other lamps you don't want. Actually, you don't want any of them but since they are cheap and Dave's envelopes say *yes*, you buy the dumb lamps in the box. This was the first time in my life I didn't have to screw the lamp pole together or unfold a fake cheap lamp shade over a flimsy metal contraption. I never loved one of those box sets of lamps I purchased in our twenty years of marriage. But it was all I could afford or at least all I perceived that I was worthy of buying. So there I was, buying a lamp that was three times as expensive simply because I adored it. Actually, I bought three.

As you can see I was having a temper tantrum. I acted immaturely. I used to do this about once a year. Call it my annual meltdown. I didn't usually spend money, but I would abruptly leave for an hour or two. Okay—and sometimes I'd also spend money.

My husband texted me to check in. I texted him back: "I'm having a great time! I'm on a shopping spree with our tithe money. Spent $250 in Target. I'm just getting started."

He graciously responded with a simple, "I love you, Amy." Smart man.

I knew that taking the frustration of my pastor's wife life out at Target wasn't going to solve a thing. But as I stood there, hurt and lonely in the middle of the pretty lamp aisle, it seems my sound mind had taken a hike.

My little episode was short-lived.

And we still tithed that week. *Ouch.*

I must admit to you, however, that I still love those lamps. (That's just between us though, okay?)

————

It was challenging for me to attend church during one particularly difficult season. The pastorate was both our lifestyle and our calling. God had called me to be a pastor's wife when I was only a freshman in high school. I took this call seriously and I even broke up with my then boyfriend, now husband, because he wasn't feeling called into full-time ministry at that time. I desired to obey God's will for my life. It's something I wanted. Something I gladly signed up for. It wasn't that I resented the role of preacher's wife. I just didn't know it would be *this* painful.

During that chapter in our ministry, I wished many times that my husband had a "regular" job. You know, the kind where I only had to show up once a year for the annual staff Christmas party with a plate of cookies, a white elephant present, and a gift for his boss. I wanted to support my husband as *he* did *his* job. I wanted to pack his lunch, kiss him as he headed out the door, and look forward to hearing about his day after work.

But a pastor's wife role isn't like that. I'll put it this way: It can get complicated. During that season, I felt completely unqualified to fulfill what I knew God had called me to do. I felt like a disappointment to everyone, myself included.

Here is the narrative I told myself:

"I can't stand up under the mounting pressure of people's demands and harsh criticism. They will destroy me. I'm scared of church people. I need to hide. I'm not safe here. No one will protect me. I can't handle this calling. I'm a failure."

Pretty pathetic self-talk, I know.

You and I both know that there's no amount of emotional shopping that cures any of this. I was at a point in my life when I couldn't seem to stop my feelings from bossing me around. I realized that if I couldn't interrupt my thoughts and talk myself back into healthy thinking I'd live in defeat and *bitterness* the rest of my days. Deep down that day in Target, I knew that was the truth.

Do you know who else felt the same way in his own life?

Jeremiah. He was a prophet to the nation of Israel. He lived in Jerusalem which at that time was a city being overthrown. God had given fair warning to his people to get a grip on their lives and stop rejecting him. God had been gracious and forgiving over and over again. Yet they refused to listen; so now they faced the consequence of their rebellious actions. Judgment came and it came hard and heavy. The book of Lamentations tells the story of Jerusalem's captivity.

The city had come to absolute ruin. Dead bodies littered the streets. Children were starving to death. Mothers were forced to choose which child would live and which would die. Cannibalism became a viable option. In the midst of this hell on earth Jeremiah said the following words. Read them carefully. Hear his desperate heart:

> *My eyes overflow with tears. No one is near to comfort*
> *me. The Lord is like an enemy. My eyes fail from*
> *weeping. I am in torment within. I am a man who*
> *has seen affliction. God has driven me away. He has*
> *turned his hand against me again and again all*
> *day. He has walled me in. He has weighed me down.*
> *He shuts out my prayer. He has surrounded me with*
> *bitterness and hardship.*
> *He mangled me and left me without help. He pierced*
> *my heart. He has filled me with bitter herbs. He has*
> *made my paths crooked. He has left me without*
> *help. He has broken my teeth; he has trampled me*
> *in the dust. I have been deprived of peace; I have*
> *forgotten what prosperity is. So I say, "My splendor*
> *is gone and all that I have hoped for from the Lord."*
> *My soul is downcast within me.*
>
> — LAMENTATIONS 2 & 3

Suffice it to say Jeremiah's life stunk big time. If he could have turned in his two week notice, I think he would have. But he couldn't. Throwing in the towel wasn't an option. Neither was escaping the pain.

Ever felt that way? Stuck in a situation you can't get out of ? Drowning in utter hopelessness?

When Jeremiah signed up for this Prophet gig I'm sure this is not what he thought it would entail. I bet he thought it would go better than it was going, I bet he didn't think his calling would be *this* painful. This was one of those difficult seasons when he too, felt like a failure. When he felt like it was all just too much. He wasn't sure he had what it would take to hang in there. He didn't know if he would make it through alive. He wasn't sure where God was or why he seemed so mean, so distant, so uninvolved, so uncaring.

What intrigues me the most is what Jeremiah said next. After venting his feelings raw before God Jeremiah courageously continues on: "Yet this I call to mind and therefore I have hope. Because of the Lord's great love, we are not consumed, for His compassions never fail. They are new every morning. Great is your faithfulness. So I say to myself, the lord is my portion therefore I will wait for Him." (Lamentations 3:21-23)

In the midst of that horror, right in that very black, pain-filled, airless space, that was Jeremiah's self-talk. Not "poor me" or "why me" or "I don't deserve this." Nothing like that.

This is one of my favorite verses in the entire Bible. I'm pretty sure it's because a man is talking to himself. I find that comforting because: 1) it means I'm not the only one who has conversations with myself and 2) men do it too. That makes me smile.

What are you currently saying to yourself? Like, really? What do you hear your own voice saying? We listen to what we say to ourselves more than any other voice. What we say to ourselves matters—profoundly.

Jeremiah decided to say something back to himself. He called good things, true things, helpful things, hope-filled things, and victorious things out from the depths of his distraught mind. He chose to declare truth even though his feelings and his reality were screaming something entirely different. He wasn't seeing God's compassions yet he declared God compassionate. He wasn't seeing God's faithfulness yet he spoke out loud that God's faithfulness was, in fact, great. He wasn't seeing evidence of God's love but not only did he say God loves, but he said God's love is *great*.

He declared that this nightmare that concerned him would not consume him. He decided to find the hope that he said moments ago he had lost. He found it by saying it. He got it back because he spoke it back. Jeremiah defeated defeat with the power of his mindset and the power of his spoken words.

I *have* hope. I am *not* consumed. I call to *my* mind. I say to *myself*.

Notice that no one else said these inspirational words *to* Jeremiah. He talked to his *own* mind and told it what to think. He took responsibility for his own sanity, his own mental health, his own emotional wellbeing, and his own spiritual vitality. He took ownership of his life. He decided in that moment that neither his circumstance nor his feelings would be in charge. He would be.

God invites us to do the same, you know. To tell our own frazzled minds precisely what to think. Today, for example, I spent an hour in bed emotionally and spiritually paralyzed. It took an all-out fight for me to not let defeat *defeat me*. Forcing myself out of bed was the first step, even though I didn't feel like getting out of bed. Opening my computer to write was the next, even though I didn't feel like writing. Not letting my feelings boss my life around is paramount, and so is learning to talk back to my feelings. My feelings won't have the final word over my day. My feelings almost always catch up. They tend to lag behind right decisions is all and I have learned to make peace with that.

Sweet friend, I don't know what battles you have in your precious head, but I do know this: If Jeremiah can do it, under the circumstances he faced, then so can we. I'm not minimizing your pain. What makes your pain painful is that it's yours. Comparing pain is pointless. Even when we know our pain is light compared to what someone else experiences, we still must walk our own road. There's no need to feel guilty over the hard spots in your life. They are hard, because they belong to you.

> *We demolish lies and every speculation that sets itself*
> *up against the knowledge of God, and take captive*
> *every thought to make it obedient to Christ.*

> — 2 CORINTHIANS 10:5

"Demolish," "take captive," and "make obedient" are all actions. They don't sound the least bit passive or easy to me. Rather, they sound strong and victorious. I'm pretty sure God wants his girls to be strong and victorious, don't you think?

This will take more intention, more resolve, and more sweat. Demolishing something is serious business. It means more than stopping it. It means pulverizing it into oblivion. It means destroying it with absolute resolve. That's what God is telling us to do when lies come into our brain. We must get serious about this or we will live in despair for the rest of our days. God tells us to take captive every thought. In other words, be the boss and hold every single thought hostage like you own the place. Like you believe your life of abundance and peace largely depends on what's going on in your head, because it most certainly does. Make those thoughts obedient. Remember, the road we are on is headed somewhere. I want *beauty* to be my destination.

Nothing changed in Jeremiah's external life. He only changed how he was speaking to himself and to God. Worship became his weapon—his weapon against the devil, his weapon against defeat, his weapon against lies and hopelessness.

I have a sign in my kitchen that says "Worship is my Weapon". Girls, take that to the spiritual bank. It works. Not just some of the time, *all* of the time. And it works like nothing else can. Just don't waste a quarter of a century, like I did, trying to figure out another way. If you walk past my house in the morning when the windows are open you will likely hear this God's girl worshiping at the top of her little lungs; you will hear me crying out to God on behalf of the people I love; you will hear me boldly reciting scripture and praying God's Word like I believe He can actually do what is written on its pages. It's my road to *sweetness* and, frankly, sanity. It's my weapon against the enemy.

I wish I could tell you that Jeremiah stayed in a positive state of mind and that everything worked out peachy for him from then on. But I can't. He faced ups and downs and setbacks like we all do. He faced more days of more tough stuff. He ranted and poured out his raw soul. He knew God could handle it. At the end of the sad book of Lamentations, he said, "You, O Lord, reign forever. Your throne endures from generation to generation."

Yes, Jeremiah, He sure does. He reigns forever. No matter what life throws at us, we do not need to fear. God reigns and his dominion endures. If all we have hoped for from the Lord is gone, we can still have hope. Hope is always wrapped up in being wrapped up with Him. Jeremiah taught us that much.

And you know what? I think he would be proud of us. I mean we have survived a lot, haven't we? Yet here we are still chugging air and seeking God. Way to go, girlfriend! Seriously, I'm proud of you. God is too.

Thanks to Jeremiah's inspiration, here's the new narrative I'm speaking to myself these days:

"God will give me strength to handle what he has called me to do. I'm in this position of influence which is a privilege and a responsibility. I can take the heat that comes with it. God has equipped me to take the bad right along with the good. I'm called to serve alongside of my husband and to be his helpmate. God is my reward. He's my defender. I'm okay regardless of what other people do, think, or say. I'm not a failure. I'm God's girl. He's proud of me. I can rest secure."

Whether you see tangible evidence of all that you have hoped for from the Lord, you can know with absolute certainty that He is involved in your life. He is faithful. He is compassionate. He is loving. You may need to come up with a new narrative you say to yourself about your life, as well. Reframe what you're going through. It helps.

Leah likely had this narrative most of her life:

"Woe is me. I'm unloved. Twenty years ago my father ruined my life. I have to share a husband with my sister. That stinks. Her kids are total brats too. And that stupid coat that Joseph wears . . . why didn't Jacob give my sons a coat? He favors Rachel's kids over mine. It's not fair that my sister is more beautiful than I am."

Here's Leah with a captive mind and a new narrative:

"I'm a blessed woman. I get to be mom to seven kids. I get to do life with my sister. Sure, that's hard sometimes, but also such a gift. My sons have a great dad. He has his hands full but I know he loves each of his children and is doing the best he can. I'm provided for and have all that I need. I don't like all the chapters of my life but I do know God is a good writer and he is writing a good story in my life. He has turned my sadness into rejoicing. I have so much to be grateful for."

You know, had Leah reframed her narrative I wonder if her sons would not have thrown Joseph into the pit. You can bet your bootstraps Leah fueled the resentment and jealousy her sons had towards their brother. Our words and our mindsets matter significantly.

Will you commit to saying things to yourself that will restore hope and peace to your soul? What about your concerns? Are they consuming you so that your sanity is slipping? If so, let's say this out loud together, okay? (It may save you from an unnecessary temper tantrum shopping spree. If you're married, I'm pretty sure your husband will be grateful for that.)

"Yet this I *call to mind* and therefore I have hope. Because of the Lord's great love, I am not consumed, for his compassions never fail. They are new every morning. Great is your faithfulness. *I say to myself,* the Lord is my portion, I will wait for Him."

That sounds like a delightful way to grow into a woman of *beauty*, wouldn't you say?

Now, excuse me while I go make my bed—the one I crawled out of to write this chapter.

P.S. A status update on my feelings . . . they eventually did catch up.

———

**Choosing Sweetness: Going Deeper with God**

*Why are you downcast oh my soul? Put your hope in God.*

— PSALMS 42:5

*Though He brings grief, He will show compassion, so great is His unfailing love. For He doesn't willingly bring affliction or grief to the children of men.*

— LAMENTATIONS 3:32-33

*Praise the Lord, oh my soul. O Lord my God, you are very great; you are clothed with splendor and majesty.*

— PSALM 104:1

- What touches you about Jeremiah's story?
- What concerns do you have? Are you allowing your concerns to consume you in some way?
- What does your self-talk sound like? Do you believe you have the power to choose how you talk to yourself?
- Is there another way you can frame what you're going through?
- What attributes of God can you declare over your life right now even if you don't currently see evidence of them?

———

SWEET NUGGETS: TAKEAWAYS TO REMEMBER

*What concerns me does not need to consume me.*

*What makes my pain painful is that it belongs to me.*

*I will live in defeat if I do not interrupt my mind and talk back to it.*

*Even if I feel like all I have hoped for from the Lord is gone, I absolutely still can have hope.*

*My feelings will have to catch up.*

*Worship is my weapon.*

# 5

# HE GAVE ME WHAT I DID NOT KNOW
# I WOULD NEED

*I* didn't want to meet *her*—the woman who would become the new woman of *my* home.

Okay, that kind of came out weird.

Let me explain.

We were selling our home. The grey one with the red front door. I know, it's hard to keep up with this nomad life of ours. We had to sell the house that God blessed us with after we lost The Yellow House. (I know. Such a big, fat, royal bummer.) Ten years after moving in, it was time to move out. I didn't want to leave. I wasn't ready to give it back yet. I wasn't ready to move to another brand new state where we didn't know a soul again. Cutting our roots off that had grown ten years deep sounded dreadful and terrifying. But, like it or not and ready or not, it was happening.

We did family life under the roof of our Grey House. We tucked our kids into their beds in those upstairs bedrooms. Every night without fail, as Cory and I walked down the hallway and back down those hardwood steps with all their familiar creaks, we would shout this little ditty to each of our kids, starting with our son, Drew:

Me: "I love you, Drew."

Drew: "I love you, Mom."

Cory: "I love you, Drew."

Drew: "I love you, Dad."

We repeated the same with our two daughters.

That's what we did every night for ten years in the grey house that was *our* family's home.

God was telling me that I had to let it go. I had to let another woman be the mom and the wife in our house. She would bring her kids, her belongings, and her traditions and start *their* life in *our* family's home. As if we never existed, as if this place didn't matter to us, and as if we never graced its doors.

I am sentimental, a little dramatic, and I place a high value on traditions. Can you tell?

I knew one thing. I couldn't meet *her*, whoever *her* would end up being. I told my husband that I did *not* want to meet these people. *Pretty please, don't make me.* Since we were selling our home by owner, our agreement was that my husband would do the showings and I'd vacate the premise. The truth is, my husband wouldn't *allow* me to be there even if I *wanted* to be there. Considering the fact that I'm banned from our own garage sales, this made sense. It seems that I have a propensity to give everything away, even valuable things, free of charge, at which point my financially wise man concludes that we would have been better off had we collected a tax deduction by dropping it all off at Goodwill.

So no one would blame my man from banning me from our house. He had all the prior evidence he needed to back the notion that I had it in me to outright give our house away. We couldn't afford to be quite *that* generous. Unless we were prepared to be homeless. Which I wasn't, and because I like homes as much as I do, you're probably not surprised. This whole agreement was a win-win for both of us.

Oh, but then there's God.

He cracks me up sometimes.

We were having a showing in an hour and a half. My husband needed to run a quick errand. He promised to be back in plenty of time. I promised to leave the premises in plenty of time so we wouldn't end up homeless.

I was in our basement when the doorbell rang. You saw that coming, didn't you? I heard my daughter answer the door. Shoot. It was *them!* The people I couldn't meet and my man agreed that I'd never have to. They were—*gulp*—an hour and a half early. They were in *my* house. *Wait a minute. Maybe my husband was behind an hour and a half?* I didn't know who to be mad at. So I was mad at all of them. I couldn't hide. They were going to be looking at every square inch of our home. I had nowhere to go, other than our chest freezer, which I didn't think was the wisest of options.

I walked up the basement steps, mumbling under my breath the entire way. I don't curse but my mumbling did include some Christian swear words. You know, the kind where you don't say the real bad word, but rather a *version* of the bad word that you *would* say if you weren't so saved.

I opened our basement door, already embarrassed about looking frazzled.

There *she* was.

The woman who was going to take our home. And along with it, all our traditions and our memories.

I took a deep breath and welcomed them in with as much warmth as I could muster. I did a pretty good job of explaining that my husband would be home shortly to give them the tour that I wasn't allowed to give them since I'd give them our house for free and my husband wouldn't like that very much . . . just kidding. We waited in the living room for my now very in-trouble husband to come home.

We began talking. This young couple was so happy. They were excited about raising their kids here in *our* home. They talked about all the things that they liked, including *our* flower gardens, *our* big backyard and *our* raspberry patch that we planted and nurtured. (By the way, the raspberry patch was my husband's favorite. He planted those himself and tended to them every summer. Picking raspberries was a therapeutic part of his day. I kind of think it had more to do with free food. Wait—I take that back. It had *everything* to do with free food.)

This stranger told me that my home was her dream home and she always wanted it. *Hey, me too. That's exactly how I feel.* She said she looked at our house every time she drove by and desired to live here one day. They called within minutes of us putting the For Sale sign in our yard.

God did something miraculous in me in those minutes that were never ever supposed to have happened in the first place.

In an unexpected detour in my heart, I began entering into her joy and stopped processing everything in the frame of my loss.

I didn't think that was possible. I actually couldn't help but like her. She was as sweet as could be. And I loved that she loved my home. I held her baby and could envision him running around the house and tromping up and down the stairs—*their* stairs. Maybe his mom would say she loved him on her way down those hardwood steps every night with the same creaks that would be there while her kids grew up in this house too.

She pointed things out to her husband that she planned on doing to the house. She did so with the mindset that it was already hers. She wasn't admiring my home or complimenting my taste but rather claiming her space. I almost felt like I was intruding. In that moment, my house was no longer my family's home. It was no longer where we belonged.

And somehow, I felt at peace about it all.

That Grey House with the red front door was a gift from God for ten wonderful happy family raising years but it was time to give it back. Right then that's what I felt God saying. God didn't owe me my dream home forever.

Funny how we think that if God blesses us with something that he can never take it back or ask us to pass it on. When we receive something we want, we want it. Like, forever. At least I do.

My man finally returned. On time, but an hour late. He had confused the time and it was true it was his fault all along. God had already taught me to believe Him rather than blame man, but you know that look that wives give their husbands when all isn't so well but you don't want to make a scene for the entire world to see? I gave him *that* look. Yes siree, I sure did.

As I was leaving the house per our prior agreement, the husband said, "Oh, am I parked in your way?" I responded, "No, even if you are, I can drive around your car onto our lawn."

Then I stopped cold in my tracks. I turned back around with a smile and said, "I mean your lawn. I should ask you. Do you mind if I drive my car on your lawn?"

We all chuckled with the irony of it all. At that moment my home was slipping away from my hands and into theirs. It no longer belonged to me. It was in their hearts and she had plans for their family's future there. Our family's time had come to an end. I didn't know where our new home would be or what it would look like or if I'd love it just as much. But I did know God was asking me to give my home away. So I did. But my husband did make sure we charged them for it. No worries—we aren't homeless.

I left with a skip in my step. I was ready. I still wasn't happy to walk away from our family's home, and it still made me very sad overall. But at least this new woman was no longer the enemy. She was no longer faceless. Meeting *her* had actually set my bundled up heart free. God invited me to feel what I didn't think I could feel: happiness for her. She said this is their forever home. Perhaps it's a gift she will get to keep. I hope she will.

———

How does God know what I need? And how is He so specific with it? How does He know exactly what to give at exactly the right time, even when what He is giving me is something I think for the life of me I do not want?

Sometimes it takes retrospection to see it, or sometimes we get to see it right away. This was one of those see it right away times for me. He confused the showing time in order to give me what I needed but what I tried hard to avoid. He loves me *that* much. And He loves you that much too. God is good at what He does.

Next time you experience something you have worked yourself silly trying so hard to avoid, take a deep breath, fix your frazzled hair, try not to swear, and remember that perhaps God knows you really *do* need the thing you don't think you want. Lean in, dear sister. It will be okay. In the process you might be surprised and delighted to have your little heart set free. There was only one way that was going to happen for me in this situation. God made sure I didn't miss the appointment. He made sure *she* didn't, either.

Since I know you might be curious, I will tell you that in leaving that house we went from an acre-sized private (like sunbathe-in-your-birthday-suit-if-you-would-like-to kind of private) lot with a beautiful relaxing nightly sunset view, to a corner postage stamp-sized lot with not one square inch of privacy. Our kid's bedrooms are about a third the size of what they were. I have no sunroom, no craft room, no formal living or dining room, and certainly no sunset views. Our home isn't unique. Count to four and there's the same version of our house all over again down the street in a different color. No raspberries. No gardens. No front porch.

But guess what? We love it.

God surprised me, yet again. Home truly is about who you share it with. We have spent more time on our tiny patio than we ever did in our expansive one at our dream home. We enjoy watching people walk by. We like the activity. We like saying hello to the entire neighborhood. I actually don't mind everyone seeing what I'm doing as I work to create a flower bed from scratch. I'm used to it now and I like the company.

And as far as sunbathing in your birthday suit goes, it's overrated and probably a health hazard, anyway. But I *am* known to enjoy a cup of coffee on my deck in my robe . . .

I will pick wildflowers on the side of the road until my garden is mature enough to produce our own cut flowers. I put up a chalkboard on the back of our house so that our neighbors can be encouraged with weekly quotes. Since a sidewalk lines the entire length of our house, I put two Adirondack chairs together with a sign that says, "Rest Awhile," and I mean it. I want neighbors to always feel welcome

We really like where we live. Who knew you can let go of your dream home, move into a not-so-dreamy home, and still be content and happy? Please don't give brick and mortar, sticks, and stones (or mice and green carpet) that much power over your life. (On second thought . . . *do* give mice that much power.) If you're not happy in the home you have now, you won't be happy in a dream home. That much I can promise you. It won't deliver joy and satisfaction. Not if you need it to.

It's good to enjoy all the gifts God delights us with. Soak them up and be grateful. Love it while you have it. But always hold the gifts you have been given with open hands. Be willing to give them back. You need not be afraid. When God has something else for you, and even if that something else isn't *as* good as what you gave up, you can still have joy abundantly. You will find new delights. You will see new gifts and blessings, I promise. The gifts God has delighted you with may be different from mine. It may be a possession, a privilege, or a position. It could be a relationship or a resource. Be grateful for the time you have it while at the same time don't be afraid to give it back if God asks you to.

I'm grateful for the lessons of the Yellow House, the gift of the Dreamy Grey House, and now the simple joys of our Cookie Cutter House on the Corner. Make that a *sweet* corner.

Make your house a home and realize that *you*, not *it*, hold the power to make it a dreamy place to come home to. Thank you, God, for giving me what I didn't know I needed, for *not* giving me what I thought I wanted, and for knowing all along exactly what I needed after all.

You are entirely amazing. I love you back.

------

## CHOOSING SWEETNESS: GOING DEEPER WITH GOD

> *Godliness with contentment is great gain. For we brought nothing into this world and we can take nothing out of it. But if we have food and clothing we will be content with that. People who want to get rich fall into temptation and a trap and into many foolish and harmful desires that plunge men into ruin and destruction . . .*
>
> *Command those who are rich in this present world not to be arrogant nor to put their hope in wealth, which is so uncertain, but to put their hope in God, who richly provides us with everything for our enjoyment. Command them to do good, to be rich in good deeds and to be generous and willing to share.*

> *In this way they will lay up treasure for themselves*
> *as a firm foundation for the coming age, so that*
> *they may take hold of the life that's truly life.*

> — 1 TIMOTHY 6:6-19

- Are there any gifts God has given you that He may be asking you to release back to Him or give away?
- Is God trying to actually set you free by asking you to enter into a situation that you're afraid of or resisting?
- What does your happiness hinge on?
- Name three blessings about your current home.

----

## SWEET NUGGETS: TAKEAWAYS TO REMEMBER

*God knows exactly what to give me at exactly the right time.*

*Enjoy the gifts God gives, but be ready to give them back.*

*If I'm not happy in the home I have now, I won't be happy in my dream home.*

*God knows what I can handle better than I do.*

*My heart gets set free when I stop resisting what He is trying to accomplish.*

6

## CHEER HER ON

*D*o you have that one friend who you think has an *in* with God?

You kinda wonder if she's like his favorite kid or something. Which makes you feel like you're not.

Which—let's all admit it—is no fun.

Her life seems perfect. She has everything *dreamy*. God answers all of *her* prayers. It sure seems like it, anyway. Not only that, but she receives the answers to *your* prayer requests. Meanwhile, you're still asking, still waiting, and still heartbroken....

Secretly, you wish something would go wrong for her— nothing extreme or anything—but some sort of tiny little hiccup would suffice. If she received even the slightest of disappointments it would make you feel oh-so-much better.

Especially when it comes to her kids. *That* hits you the hardest. Her kids soar through life while your kids have countless struggles. (Or maybe you desire desperately to be a mom yet find yourself battling infertility, while your friend is a baby-making machine.) Perhaps, your friend has a daughter who excels at everything. Her family is in constant celebration mode, while you cry yourself to sleep because your teenage daughter is in her room doing the same. A fruit snack, a hug, and a Disney movie don't fix things anymore. Those simple days of childhood are long gone.

A mother is only as happy as her saddest child. When our kids hurt, we hurt. Their heartache becomes our heartache. This is motherhood. It takes a lot out of us. We feel everything our children feel. No wonder why celebrating the wins feels so good. We'd just like more of them. Right? That friend in your life who seems to have it all together, especially when it comes to her kids, it hits you in a tender place in your heart. Everything seems perfectly peachy for her while so much feels painful for you.

So here's my question: How do we celebrate with *her* when she has everything we desire and are asking God for?

It's easy to celebrate with someone over things we don't care about. When *their* thing isn't *our* thing we can rejoice when they rejoice. *No problemo.* But when their success and joy intersects with our grief and heartache? Hold on, girlfriend, that's a whole different ball game.

You know who else understood these feelings? Jesus's Aunt Elizabeth, or as I like to call her, Liz.

> *In the time of Herod king of Judea there was a priest named Zechariah . . . his wife Elizabeth was also a descendant of Aaron. Both of them were upright in the sight of God, observing all the Lord's commandments and regulations blamelessly. But they had no children because Elizabeth was barren, and they were both well along in years.*
>
> — LUKE 1:5-7

You can read Luke Chapter 1 for the full low down. I will summarize for you in case you're anything like me in that I seldom put down a book to go get my Bible when an author asks me to do so. I got you.

Elizabeth was barren for most of her life, which caused her tremendous heartache. In her old age she finally became a mom to John the Baptist. He was the guy who would grow up in the wilderness eating locusts and wild honey as he prepared himself to prepare a way for the long-awaited Messiah. Liz's teenage niece, Mary, would be chosen as the mother of that long-awaited one, Jesus Christ. Jesus was Liz's niece's son.

Did you follow that? In other words, this was a perfect set up for Liz to wrestle with comparison and jealousy.

Liz lived a shame-filled life full of disgrace. According to the practice of the day, her husband had a right to divorce her because she didn't have any children. She endured ridicule and judgement because it was believed a barren woman was cursed because of sin. Liz knew that not having any children would mean a hopeless, helpless, poverty-stricken life in their elderly years. There was an aching longing in her heart to be a mom. It was real, it was hard, and it felt unfair.

Her heartache continued for decade after decade. In the midst of those barren years, Liz had no idea what the purpose of that pain would be. She prayed, waited, asked, and grieved. She likely felt forgotten and disregarded by God at times through those years of longing.

Do you think Liz looked at her female relatives who got the privilege of being mothers or all the neighbor ladies around town who were busy in their homes, cooking for their families and having tea parties with their daughters, and thought that maybe that meant that God loved *them* more? That they were his favorites and she was not? Do you think she asked, "Why them, God? Why not me?" Deep pain and confusion were her steady, daily companions for close to a lifetime.

We have the privilege of knowing the end of Liz's story within two minutes of reading the beginning, but remember that *she* didn't have that same luxury. When it comes to our own stories, none of us do. We live our lives first, not knowing how the end of our story will be written until we get there. Then at the end, we see everything more clearly. When it's over we understand most of what we couldn't understand while walking through it. It was no different for Elizabeth.

Hindsight never comes until the season is over, the answer is given, or the pain has been endured. A *grown up* woman of God has learned she doesn't need hindsight in order to walk in peace. She doesn't wait for it in order to trust God's goodness and faithfulness over her life and maybe most importantly over her children's lives.

I wished I'd have known this twenty years ago when Cory had just started his very first full-time ministry job as a youth pastor. We quickly fell in love with our students as well as the entire congregation. And we were loved in return. We thought that was a good thing. The senior pastor and his wife did not.

Opportunities for my husband to fill the pulpit dwindled. We were told not to greet people in the foyer and that we should go outside following the service instead. So we did. But it seemed that was a problem too. We were then told to stay in the sanctuary until everyone left. We weren't allowed to visit people in the hospital unless they were personal friends but even then we were instructed to not pray or read scripture. We couldn't visit shut-ins even if we were in their neighborhood.

The pastor didn't want the congregation confused as to who the pastor was, he reasoned. And I wasn't allowed to attend women's events. That was the *senior* pastor's wife's territory. I could only interact with students. One day the pastor's wife rang my doorbell, she said this when I opened the front door, "If your husband can't get the youth ministry to grow we don't need him here."

During that painfully confusing experience it felt like God was punishing us, that He wasn't pleased with us, and that He had forgotten us. Ten years later we would gain the hindsight we needed to see that God was actually preparing us for what He had *for* us. Cory would become a senior pastor which would mean I'd be the senior pastor's wife. God gave us a serious whooping so we would know how *not* to behave. He scarred us with wounds inflicted by insecure, territorial leaders so that one day those scars would become reminders. Reminders to do things differently. God was preparing us for what he had planned for us.

It took ten years before the hindsight came. The pain eventually made sense. Someday, it would all make sense to Liz too. Someday, she would see that God had picked her for profound purposes, he had not been punishing her. She would see that her God had not forgotten her, he had things *for* her. The delay was intentional. God needed other things to fall into place first. God *does* have more going on than our beating hearts. We do realize that, right? The world doesn't revolve around us. We matter—significantly so. But God does orchestrate the events of the *entire* universe. So maybe we can learn to live with a pinch more patience towards Him.

Luke tells us that Elizabeth was upright in the sight of God. Even though God wasn't giving her what she begged him for, she behaved blamelessly rather than *bitterly*. Liz was growing into a *beautiful* woman.

You know what? I think God would have loved to have sent her a note saying:

"Liz, I need a couple of more decades. I'm not ready to send my son yet. I want your son to blaze a trail for my son. So you will need to wait for my timing. Trust me. I see you. I have not forgotten you. I'm pleased with you. I'm not mad at you. I have chosen you, not ignored you. My heart aches along with yours. It does. But I have something pretty big going on here. I need more time. Your son will make a way for mine. I love you. I know what I'm doing. Keep loving me here in this place while you wait. Will you do that for me? Love me still. Stay standing upright, sweet daughter of mine."

Elizabeth's blessing eventually did come in her old age:

> *The angel said to him: "Do not be afraid, Zechariah;*
> *your prayer has been heard. Your wife Elizabeth*
> *will bear you a son, and you are to call him John.*
> *He will be a joy and delight to you, and many will*
> *rejoice because of his birth, for he will be great in*
> *the sight of the Lord . . . and he will go on before the*
> *Lord, in the spirit and power of Elijah, to turn the*
> *hearts of the parents to their children and the*
> *disobedient to the wisdom of the righteous—to make*
> *ready a people prepared for the Lord." Zechariah*
> *asked the angel, "How can I be sure of this? I am an*
> *old man and my wife is well along in years." The*
> *angel said to him, "I am Gabriel. I stand in the*
> *presence of God, and I have been sent to speak to*
> *you and to tell you this good news. And now you*
> *will be silent and not able to speak until the day this*
> *happens, because you didn't believe my words,*
> *which will come true at their appointed time."*
>
> — LUKE 1:13 - 20

Elizabeth declared, "God did this for me. He took away my pain and disgrace." (Luke 1:25)

Hold on, though. Before you think it's all peaches and cream and happily ever after . . . .

*The angel went to Mary and said to her, "Greetings you*

*who are highly favored! The Lord is with you . . .
don't be afraid Mary you have found favor with
God. You will be with child and give birth to a son
and you are to give him the name Jesus. He will be
great and be called the Son of God. The Lord God
will give him the throne . . . and he will reign . . . his
kingdom will never end . . . even Elizabeth, your
relative, is going to have a child in her old age, and
she who is said to be barren is in her sixth month.
At that time Mary got ready and hurried to a town
in the hill country of Judea, where she entered
Zechariah's home and greeted Elizabeth. When
Elizabeth heard Mary's greeting, the baby leaped in
her womb, and Elizabeth was filled with the Holy
Spirit. In a loud voice she exclaimed: "Blessed are
you among women, and blessed is the child you will
bear! But why am I so favored, that the mother of
my Lord should come to me? As soon as the sound of
your greeting reached my ears, the baby in my
womb leaped for joy. Blessed is she who has believed
that the Lord would fulfill his promises to her!"*

— LUKE 1:39 - 1:45

Do you see what is unfolding? Can you crawl through the
Bible parchment into Elizabeth's living room? This actually
happened to real, oxygen-breathing, hormone-raging women.

Liz, herself pregnant, is now taking care of the morning-sick
mother of the Messiah, who happens to be her much younger
teenage niece. No doubt the pair sat in rocking chairs talking
each other's ears off about all the things pregnant women talk
about it. I can only imagine Liz wanted to know details on how
this all unfolded in Mary's life.

Liz: "Tell me everything, Mary! What happened? How did you find out you were pregnant?"

Mary: "You've heard of the angel Gabriel, right? Well, he appeared to me out of nowhere . . . ."

Liz: "Wait, what? Like he actually talked to you? In person??"

Mary: "Yes, he talked to me face-to-face! He told me I was going to have a child through the Holy Spirit and that my son would be great and His kingdom would never end."

Liz: "Really. Wow. I don't even know what to say. That's truly amazing in every way."

Mary: "What about you, Auntie Liz—tell me everything! After all these years of waiting to become a mom, how did you find out you were pregnant? I can't wait to hear your story!"

Liz: "Oh well, it wasn't a big thing, really. Your Uncle Zachariah . . . well, suddenly he couldn't speak anymore, which was really confusing. We ended up playing a little game of charades which took about an hour and fifty guesses but I eventually figured out that he was trying to tell me I'm pregnant. It was quite anti-climatic, really. I certainly did not get an encounter with an angel."

Do you see an opportunity here for the devil to have a field day? For comparison, jealousy, resentment, and discontentment to run wild? Even in her joy over having a child, Elizabeth could have chosen to have a royal pity party, helium balloons and all, over who apparently is God's more favored daughter. Mary, a young girl who has not even lived long enough to know what an unfulfilled, lifelong longing feels like, waltzes in and one-ups Elizabeth right there in her living room. Elizabeth has been waiting for years for this moment, but Mary's news is still better. Mary steals the show.

Mary hadn't even been trying to get pregnant. If one of them was qualified, deserving, capable and worthy of mothering the Messiah, wasn't it Liz? I mean, really. If one of these women deserved a personal word from an angel of God, wasn't it the woman who had walked with God and obeyed him all her life? Elizabeth had to settle for a ridiculous charades game with her suddenly mute husband to figure out the good news for herself. Young Mary got a face-to-face experience with a divine being from Heaven.

We feel blessed until someone else comes along with a bigger blessing. We can feel content with our walk with God until someone else describes some profound moment with God that makes our time with Him seem trivial. We think that must mean we are less special, less privileged, less treasured, or less important. We might think our callings and talents matter until we line them up next to *hers*. *Her* gifting and assignment is *really* important. There must be some reason why, some way in which we are not good enough.

*God trusts her more. God loves her more. God favors her more. God picked someone other than me for a more significant purpose. I got the leftovers.*

We know we are blessed but we still can't seem to help it.

*She* has more of what I long for.

*She* got the answer to *my* prayer.

Elizabeth's son's sole purpose in life would be to serve the son in Mary's womb. Let that sink in. From the very beginning, Liz knew that her son would be insignificant compared to Mary's, and unworthy to even untie His sandals (Luke 3:16). And to top it off, he would have his head cut off and served on a platter because of his loyalty to Mary's son. This is big-girl-pants-pulled-up kind of stuff right here. (And we have an issue when our kid doesn't get the starting spot on the soccer team? Lord, have mercy.)

When Elizabeth heard Mary's greeting, the baby leapt in her womb and Elizabeth was filled with the Holy Spirit. In a loud voice she exclaimed, "Blessed are you among women, and blessed is the child you will bear! But why am I so favored that the mother of my Lord should come to me?" (Luke 1:41-43)

I can hardly get over Liz's response. It's so rare. It's beautiful and mature. She's not *bitter*. She's not jealous. She's not mad. She's happy for Mary and she proclaims a great blessing upon her son in a *loud* voice. (I love that detail.)

Who does this? Do you know an *Elizabeth*? Like, in real life? Who on this self-absorbed, social media-bragging, often critical, frequently jealous planet of ours behaves in this kind of *beautiful* way?

If you know a real life Elizabeth, buy that girl a coffee this week and thank her for being the rare bright spot she is.

Liz was content when Mary got more. When Mary was entrusted with greater significance, greater influence and bigger blessings, Liz celebrated with her. Mary received a more profound and clearly more exciting experience with God. Liz didn't seem to mind. Mary was gifted with—wait for it—a more gifted child. Nope, that didn't throw her into a hissy fit, either. Mary was given a son who would have a bigger following, bigger impact, bigger name, and greater power. Elizabeth *knew* this. She knew in that moment in her home when Mary popped through the door. My son will make a way for hers. My son will step aside for hers. Her son is the Messiah, my son is his servant. And I'm okay with that.

Can you imagine her saying, "I came this close to being the mother of The Messiah? You have got to be kidding me! This close! Why her? Why not me? Why not my son? Why not our family?"

Elizabeth didn't focus on those self-centered, peace-destroying, joy-sabotaging, childish, pity-partying thoughts. How? She had *grown up*, not just *grown old*. That's how. *Beauty* won. *Ugly* lost. God filled her in that moment with His Holy Spirit. He empowered her to respond in ways she couldn't have otherwise. Through the power of the presence of the Holy Spirit in her, she was able to respond maturely. She lived generously, graciously, selflessly, blamelessly, and uprightly because of the quiet, unseen power that rested within her.

Do you realize that we have that same Spirit in us, on us, with us, and for us too? That exact same power is available to us 24/7, 365 days a year. The Spirit of God can enable you and me to respond in ways we wouldn't be able to without Him. How often do we tap into this asset? We have access to so much power, but it often goes unused. It's the kind of power that would actually equip us do the impossible. Like cheer on people we are jealous of! Like celebrate with people when they have what we want!

The Holy Spirit is a gentleman, though. He isn't loud or domineering. He waits for an invitation from us. He waits for us to want Him. He waits for us to give him the green light to activate His power. He waits for us to realize our way isn't working. He waits for us to back off so He can step in. He is powerful, mighty, effective, and amazing. But He won't act until He receives permission from us to engage. This means He takes the floor after we take a seat.

We *can* be an Elizabeth. Oh yes, we can. The question is, will we get out of the way so the power of the Holy Spirit can flow through us and make this happen?

We get jealous of God's generosity to others. Matt 20:15 describes vineyard workers who agreed to work for a certain amount of money. The problem was they worked all day and ended up being paid the same amount of money as the workers who showed up at the end of the shift. Needless to say, drama unfolded. The owner of the vineyard said, "I'm not being unfair. Don't I have the right to do what I want with my own money? Or are you envious that I'm generous?" We would prefer to divvy out God's blessings ourselves. (And in our favor, of course.)

Whether or not we verbalize it out loud, it's tempting to give

God stipulations on how much He can bless others: "As long as other people don't get more than me, then I'm fine. Just keep it all fair, God. Or actually, if you're going to lean a little, lean slightly towards me—thank you very much! I want other people's kids to do well but I want mine to do better. They can succeed in things my kids are not involved in though—that's totally cool. I want other people to feel important, sure I do, as long as I don't feel subsequently unimportant. God, you have my permission to bless other people's homes, careers, kids, marriages, ministries, businesses, bodies, bank accounts … just not more than you bless mine."

The perfect, every-prayer-answered kind of life doesn't exist. Not even for the *Marys* in your life.

And Marys have Marys of their own. You know that, right? *You* may be someone else's Mary. Did you ever consider that? We are hyper aware of our own lack and ignorant of our extraordinary blessings. The Marys of the world have unanswered prayers too, even if it doesn't seem like it from your vantage point.

I have a Mary in my life. Her family lives close by. Her kids are growing up near their grandparents. She has roots down deep and feels like she belongs where she lives. My Mary has a darling cottage on a lake. One with lots of windows to let in the glorious view and the sunshine. A place where her family gathers to make memories and will do so for generations to come. My Mary gets to raise her kids with the same friends she started the motherhood journey with. She has perfect, clear skin that doesn't require foundation. (Her barn doesn't need paint, in other words.) She grows more vegetables than weeds in her garden. She doesn't sweat right above her lip and since she doesn't wear foundation she doesn't need to be paranoid about the mustache that seems to appear when her foundation melts off under her nose. She looks good in a messy bun. She knows how to create a chore chart for her kids and actually follows through with it for longer than two days. She cooks meals that her entire family will eat. Her bathroom sink isn't full of hair and dried up toothpaste. She manages to wash bed sheets more than once a month like you're apparently supposed to. (Oops!) She feels successful and confident all the time. She never struggles with insecurity.

I'm always aware of my lack. And very aware of what other people *don't* lack.

But maybe, just maybe, my Mary looks at me and thinks I have what she longs for.

Good grief.

Who knows?

I can turn this *ugly, bitter* place of insecurity and jealousy into a place of *sweetness*. I can get over myself and bless her anyway, like Elizabeth. I can start by saying a power-packed phrase: "I'm so happy for you and the blessing you just received! Yay!" Satan will lose his foothold over my mind if I do.

There is no secret to being an Elizabeth. We just need to do it. We need to get over ourselves so the Spirit can take over. We need to give Him permission to do His supernatural thing through us. We need to say things we may not feel like saying. This isn't hard. It's just not easy.

Support her. Cheer her on. Celebrate with her.

She has her life, you have yours. She has her blessings, you have yours. She has her gifts, you have yours. She has her home, her assignments, and her roles and so do you. What is the point of obsessing over someone else's life when doing so has no power to change your own reality?

A woman in our first church once told me she was jealous of me because I was a preacher's wife. She had dreamed of being one since she was a little girl. But, I tell you what, this woman was the best pretend pastor's wife I've ever met. She fit all the stereotypes: She played the piano, directed the children's Christmas program, taught Sunday school, visited shut-ins, sung on the worship team, hosted people for dinner, decorated the church, organized pot lucks, and led fundraisers for the youth ministry. She was living the preacher's wife life minus the being married to the preacher part. Minor detail, really.

The point is that she may not hold the title but she is doing all she dreamed of doing without it. Perhaps precisely because she doesn't hold the title. I told her:

"God *has* fulfilled your dream. This *is* God's favor on your life. You get to play the role without the burden. Zero stress of actually having the pressure of being an actual pastor's wife. You get to do the very things you envisioned yourself doing if you were her. Can you see that as a gift? No one has expectations and demands of you. What you do is a blessing, not a requirement. People are grateful for your time and sacrifice not critical that you should do more or something else entirely. You don't carry the weight of the church. You're free to love without tangled strings attached. If you have ladies over to your home they thank you and feel blessed."

I used to have groups of ladies over until I started hearing complaints about why it took me so long to have some women over. They wanted to know why they were further down my list, why I didn't have them over sooner, why I included them with the women I did instead of the women they expected to be included with. I hurt people's feelings by trying to love them, precisely because I am the preacher's wife.

With this, as with everything, there's a reason why God gives you certain things and gives other people different things. God knows how He has wired us and equipped us. He knows we may not have been created to handle what *they* have. Do we even know what we are asking God for sometimes? Are we sure we want Him to answer *that* prayer? You do know the difficult parts that come with that life, possession, job, position, or title, right? God may not have equipped me to handle the stressful stuff that would come with the good stuff I want (like owning a second home on a lake).

God's will for your life has little to do with you and it has nothing to do with the women who you think are better or more blessed than you. You're not in competition with the people next to you. Nobody took "your" spot.

God didn't compare Elizabeth and Mary. He didn't hand out bigger blessings and bigger purposes to His favorite one. He didn't evaluate who was more talented, worthy, capable or deserving. God needed a woman to be the mother of His son, so He created Mary. He needed a woman to be the mother of His son's forerunner, so He created Elizabeth. That's all there is to it. No comparison, no competition. Simply God's perfect design for His precious daughters with His kingdom purposes in mind.

Elizabeth didn't have all that Mary had but she did have all that God wanted her to have, you can be assured of that. And you know what? She enjoyed it. She saw herself as a blessed woman. She knew she was loved by God. Mary wasn't a threat to Elizabeth. She was *that* secure. Which is why Elizabeth was able to bless Mary.

There isn't a woman on this planet who is a threat to you. Start believing that and you too, will be freed up to be an Elizabeth to your Mary . . . and wouldn't that just be the happiest of days!

———

CHOOSING SWEETNESS: GOING DEEPER WITH GOD

*A heart at peace gives life to the body but envy rots the bones.*

— PROVERBS 14:30

*He who refreshes others will himself be refreshed.*

— PROVERBS 11:25

*Do nothing out of selfish ambition or vain conceit but
in humility consider others better than yourselves.
Each of you should look not only to your own
interests but also to the interests of others.*

— PHILIPPIANS 2:2-4

*Resentment kills a fool and envy slays the simple.*

— JOB 5:2

- Do you have a Mary in your life?
- Do you have prayers that seem to go unanswered for you but not for others?
- How can you cheer people on who have what you long to have?
- Are there any places of insecurity in your heart because you're comparing yourself, your role, or your blessings to someone else's?

———

SWEET NUGGETS: TAKEAWAYS TO REMEMBER

*God has not forgotten me. He has things for me.*

*God is not punishing me. He has picked me for profound purposes.*

*A grown up woman doesn't need hindsight in order to trust in God's
faithfulness in the middle of her story.*

*My Mary doesn't really have everything, anyway. God is too good and too wise to give one person everything.*

*Nobody took my "spot."*

*I will be freed up when I don't view other women as threats.*

*I can be an Elizabeth to my Mary.*

# 7

# I WILL BE OKAY

*W*e pulled into our driveway after a long weekend away.

Right then, I knew.

An instant lump formed in my throat. Grief welled up in my heart.

In the yard next to ours, I saw my neighbor—but not just any neighbor. This neighbor was also my friend, my prayer partner, and a fellow stay-at-home mom. She was the older sister I never had. She was the lender of all things "kitcheny" that I either couldn't find in my own cupboards, didn't have in the first place, or just plain forgot to buy when I went to the store that morning even though it was on my list. (Please tell me I'm not the only one.)

When I saw her, she was knee deep in mulch, sprucing up her landscaping. I tried to reason with myself that perhaps with a daughter graduating and an open house fast approaching she was simply tidying up the place.

But I knew better. Something was wrong.

My neighbor kept an immaculate home. It was spotless, military-style perfection. All. The. Time. (I'm not exaggerating about the military part—she's an Air Force veteran.) But landscaping, weed pulling, and flower bed-fussing? Let's just say that's not quite her cup of tea. There was a little patch of what I suppose used to be a beautiful flower bed between our yards. Years ago thick weeds took over, and who knows what all was lurking in there. My son's basketball ended up in those weeds a million times. No one cared. I never worried about a ricocheting ball breaking off a much beloved daisy or flattening a tender Hosta plant.

So when I saw her out fussing with her landscaping, the landscaping she never cared one smidgen about before, I knew.

She was moving away.

Later that evening a knock on our door confirmed my dreadful suspicion. She and I spent the next several hours on my front porch swing. I sobbed ugly tears. The kind when you use your sleeve as a Kleenex, like a kindergartener would do, and just don't give a darn. We held hands, we cried, we prayed, we reminisced.

She was leaving me.

As my next door neighbor, we shared a huge backyard, but we also shared our lives. We shared our spices, ladders, crock pots, rakes, books, trampoline, garden produce, and jewelry. (I know, how fun is that?) We shared our tears, our hearts, our homes, our time, our momma burdens, our Jesus, our prayers, and our very real, vulnerable, authentic selves. We gave each other perspective. We spoke truth when the other couldn't see it for herself.

My neighbor was the most capable woman I ever met. She inspired me. She made me a better version of myself. She taught me how to pray like I meant it. She birthed in me a greater spiritual confidence to approach the throne room of God and believe Him to do the impossible. She infused courage into my soul.

She made me meals, I made her dessert. (Let's just say we

knew what the other wasn't good at.) She cleaned out my fridge and scrubbed my utility sink spotless as a surprise while we were out of town. She stocked my fridge with food on more than one occasion so I didn't have to run to the grocery store upon returning home from vacation. (I know! Sorry if I'm giving you serious neighbor envy right about now.)

I did my best to bless her back but I never felt like I could bless her quite like she knew how to bless me. Do you have a friend like that? The one where deep down you know if you were keeping score you would be way ahead on the receiving end.

We both felt safe, loved, and secure right next to each other. Like little school girls, we once promised we wouldn't move without the other. We talked about staying in this community where neither of us had family or roots until it was time for both of our families to move. We hoped that day would never come. But it did and she broke her promise. Secretly, we both knew one of us would. It was a cute little pinky promise but one we couldn't keep.

That evening when I saw her in the mulch and she broke the news to me on my front porch, we talked late into the evening. Just she and I, giving life advice, speaking words of encouragement, saying every little thing we could think of that the other just might need down the road. We tucked those gifts of words in our back pockets like they were precious treasures. Middle age and several moves already in the books for each of us also taught us that no matter how much we meant to each other, distance would change things. We wouldn't stay in touch like we wished we could. As if we would never see each other again, we imparted everything we thought the other may need for the next season of her life. I was scared of living life without my kindred spirit right next door.

We were like two girls who had just spent a week at camp with our new forever BFF and now the inevitable goodbye was waiting. As she was about to make the fifty foot walk back to her home, she turned to me and said four little words:

"You will be okay."

I didn't believe her.

I rested my weary head in my hands and sobbed.

We all have intersections in our life when we are convinced we won't be okay. When a parent enters hospice, we know it won't be long until we face life without them. When our first child is about to start kindergarten, we are convinced we won't be able to keep it together as we let them go. When our youngest leaves home for college, the silent empty nest looms loud in our soul. When our son says, "I do," we know he is no longer ours.

When a layoff is inevitable, when we know the side effects of chemotherapy are about to begin, when the divorce papers are about to be finalized, when our infertility doctor is out of answers, when we are out of options and have to face the reality of life head on, we doubt if we will be okay.

*I'm not going to be okay this time. Not through this.*

Before our last move, I begged my husband for one thing. It wasn't a bigger house or new furniture (though that would have been swell). There was one thing that was a non-negotiable to my heart: I wanted to move together as a family. When we loaded up our life in a U-Haul, I wanted all five of us to go *together*.

Our son Drew was a senior in high school when the reality of a move was on the table. It was February. College started in August. I thought my request was very doable. I needed us to all move to Kansas City for a few months, a few weeks even, *together*. I didn't want to even consider transitioning our family to a new city in a new state without our family being complete. It was heartbreaking enough to send our son off to college eight hours away. I wanted us, even for a brief time, to sleep under a new roof in a strange home and find our way around an unfamiliar city as a family unit together. I wanted my son to know where home was.

That didn't happen. We packed up our belongings from our family home and we stuck them in a moving truck, except for our son's belongings which we loaded up separately in our family van. We shut the door for the last time on the life we knew in our family home and drove our son to college the very same day.

We had to bring our son to college one day before the official freshman "Welcome Day." No welcome committee. No move in crew. No fanfare. No banners. No hoopla. No fun activities. Just one kid and his parents who had to beg the college to let them drop their son off a day early so they could get their other two kids to their first day of high school in a new city.

Who does this? What kind of parents were we? I felt like such a loser. Everything had been falling apart for weeks. Delays in closing on our new home, complications with the sale of our own, trying to get our daughters enrolled in time to attend a new school without a home address. It was a disaster. Everything that could go wrong did.

We left our son in a sterile cement-walled room in an eerily quiet hall that looked more like a prison than a home. He didn't know a soul on the campus. Well, we did meet a student Resident Assistant from another floor, but he seemed less than excited to start fulfilling his role a day sooner than he was scheduled to do so.

We said goodbye and left our son.

We drove five hours back to Iowa to pick up our daughters and drove through the night to Kansas City. We checked into a hotel at 2:00 a.m. School started the next day. Nothing like taking that first day of school picture in front of room #302 of the Hampton Inn. We Googled our new home address to give to our daughters so they could *find* home after their first day at a brand new high school.

This wasn't how it was supposed to go.

God didn't give me the *one* thing I begged him for. I really believed he would give it to me too. I wasn't asking for much. In the grand scheme of life, I realize this scenario isn't a huge deal. No one was dying. There was no actual crisis unfolding. You may think it's silly that I'd even consider this "hard." I'd agree. But you know what? The things that matter to your heart, matter. You have permission to feel. You have permission to process your life. The fact that it's your life being impacted makes it a big deal. So I guess neither one of us needs to feel like our stuff is silly.

The tears came later but in those few days of doing what we needed to do, God graciously gave us sound minds, steady spirits, smiling faces, and a boatload of serious adrenaline.

My son made it through that day alone. Three years later, he doesn't even remember that day the way I do. And Siri got our daughters to school from a hotel room. She helped them find home afterwards too. (Thanks, Siri! How did we navigate life before you?)

I didn't need all I thought I needed.

Neither did my kids.

We were okay.

Who knew we could handle it? God did.

That day when my neighbor friend broke the bad news, I held tightly to her words.

You will be okay.

I didn't know how. But we never do ahead of time, do we? We usually have no earthly idea how we will be okay, but somehow we are. At the end of each day we realize again, I was okay today. You know, I have found that anticipating difficult things usually is far more difficult than actually experiencing it.

I knew life would be so different without my neighbor. I

couldn't imagine day-to-day life in my house without my friend in hers. Her house is now occupied by someone who doesn't belong there. That's how I feel. A moving company stuffed my friend's life and our friendship into a truck and had the audacity to drive away.

But you know what? She was right. I am okay.

It's been awhile since I said goodbye to my next door neighbor friend and I still don't like it, not one bit. I'm sad sometimes, but *I am okay*. Once as I was making lasagna for a dinner party—I only make lasagna for houseguests, mind you—I caught myself heading out my door to her house. The recipe called for garlic salt and I only had garlic powder. I knew she would have some. (It was entirely possible that I actually *did* have garlic salt. I have a hard time finding spices in my unorganized, chaotic cupboards. She has hers alphabetized—of course she does. I figure it's quicker to run next door than to dig through my mess. Besides, I always loved any excuse just to say hello.)

I momentarily forgot she was no longer there. I realized my mistake as my foot landed on her front porch. I paused, sighed, spun myself around on one foot and walked across the yard back to my kitchen. I sprinkled a pinch of garlic powder instead of garlic salt in my lasagna.

It still makes me sad that she is gone but I'm finding His grace to be sufficient for yet one more season, one more change, one more transition, one more heartache, one more goodbye and one more thing I didn't receive that I thought I needed.

We keep breathing because God gives us breath. We have courage to face the tomorrows we dread because He is already there and He isn't worried. He is steady, unmoving, faithful, and in control.

The very things we dread and the pains we fear facing? God's mercies and compassion will meet us right in that very place. That's a pinky promise that you can count on. Every new morning His love covers our every new heartache. Embrace each difficult transition with a dependence on the One who will always be there. He is your unfailing steady in life.

Even when He fails to honor your declared "nonnegotiables," He will not fail you.

I regret to report that there are now happy, delicate Hosta plants where that weed patch used to be. The new neighbor seems to have a thing for gardening. My son will try to keep his basketball from steamrolling her lovely flowers and I will try to be friendly to the woman who planted them there. I suppose it's about time to tell her that if she ever needs a pinch of garlic salt that I'll be here, right next door. I may not be able to find the spice she needs and even if I do find it there's a really good chance it will be well past its expiration date but come to think of it . . . maybe she really came over just to say hello, anyway.

———

P.S. Dorothy, I love you. I miss you still. I miss our lunches and our prayers. I miss us. I will forever be grateful that our lives intersected on W. 15th St. S. for such a time. My life is richer because you lived next door. You taught me much and blessed me well. I want to be like you when I grow up. And yes, I still wonder if you really are an angel undercover. Oh, and I wore the pearls today. Thank you for sharing your jewelry box with me. Thank you for sharing your life with me. This was a taste of what's to come in heaven. By the way, I made reservations to have a room in The Mansion next to yours. Can't wait! Oh, and neither one of us will have to cook or clean! Glory!!

P.S.S. Drew, Alexis and Allie, you were incredible troopers through a very tough transition. You all impressed me. You were capable of handling way more than I even thought you could. You're brave and stouthearted warriors. While I feel bad that as a mom I wasn't able to orchestrate things to make those days of transition easier for you, I realized that God is your true source of strength and protection, not me. I will fail you. I will come up short. But your God never will. You're capable of handling everything God puts in front of you. Live fearlessly. You will always make it through. Even when life isn't okay, you will be.

————

CHOOSING SWEETNESS: GOING DEEPER WITH GOD

*Do not fear for I am with you. Do not be dismayed, for I am your God. I will strengthen you and help you. I will uphold you with my hand.*

— ISAIAH 41:10

*Cast your care upon the Lord for He cares for you.*

— PSALM 55:22

*When I am afraid, I will trust in You.*

— PSALM 56

- Do you have a list of ultimatums or nonnegotiables you've given God?
- Are you facing a difficult circumstance and you're not sure how you will be okay?
- Do you have that one thing you've asked God for, but things are falling apart rather than falling into place?

- Thank God for the things you've survived that you didn't think you could.

———

SWEET NUGGETS: TAKEAWAYS TO REMEMBER

*I will be okay.*

*Anticipating a difficult thing is usually more difficult than experiencing it.*

*I can have courage to face the tomorrows I fear because He is already there.*

*God is my unfailing steady in life.*

*Even if he fails to honor my nonnegotiables, He won't fail me.*

# 8

# I WILL GO ON WITH HIM

*T*here are times when I have to stop reading the Bible.
Usually, it's with a sweet, surrendered sigh.

After all, a sink full of dishes is *still* there and supper has not made itself and we are out of frozen pizza and the laundry is still in a heap on the couch, but at least it's clean. (I do get a few kudos for that, right?)

The Holy Spirit gives me a little nudge to shut my Bible so I can serve my family. Most of the time, my treasured moments in God's Word are interrupted only by these usual duties of daily life.

However, if I'm being honest, I'd tell you that sometimes I stop reading because the stories in the Bible are difficult for me. There are times when my heart is deeply troubled by what the ink on its thin parchment reads. I don't know what else to do but let the tears flow and set the Word aside, closing the cover on the words I cannot seem to process. I get scared by the things God allows, the things God does, and the things His people do. The Bible sometimes brings confusion not comfort, and pain not peace.

I love the Word of God, but I do struggle with parts of it. Is it okay for me to admit that? My Sunday School teachers never warned me about these feelings. This isn't the sort of stuff we talk about in church.

I don't know how many of us are out there who feel this way, but I do know there are at least two of us. One morning, a friend and I met for coffee and I don't remember who was brave enough to broach the topic first but we went *there*. We fought through lumps in our throats and tears gently dripping off our chins as we courageously talked about this *shutting the Bible thing* we both do. Two church-going God's girls felt free enough to be honest. We knew God could handle our questions and our confusion. She drank her black coffee while I sipped my usual white chocolate mocha with a splash of hazelnut. Two different palettes, one secret struggle, and a God who gave us both permission to process it all.

We talked about the story of Abraham and Hagar. You may already know that theirs is a difficult one. This chapter won't be an easy read. You're free to skip this one, rip it out, or mark it up. However, I believe there's ground we can gain by being honest about difficult places. I'm pretty sure we will be glad we "went there" when we are through. It won't be easy on either of us but if you're willing I am too. There is a daughter of God out there who needs to hear this. (If that person isn't you, would you consider being okay with this chapter being for someone who does need it? I thank you in advance for your grace.)

In the Old Testament, Abraham (the "Father of Faith," as described in the Bible) sexually violated his slave Hagar.

There—I said it.

One day Sarah told her husband to take Hagar and that's what he did (Genesis 16). Sarah handed Hagar over to Abraham so he could impregnate her. Abraham didn't date her, court her, win her over, love her, woo her, pick her wildflowers or even send her a flirtatious text. Hagar didn't get a ring, no "save the date," no bridesmaids.

Abraham didn't *ask* Hagar. He *took her*. Let that soak in for a moment.

It was abuse.

It's hard for me to think about Abraham doing that. But Godly people can make a muddy, rainy day, filthy mess of things. I have to find room in my heart for that tension. Maybe you do too. Godly people do ungodly things. It happens a lot, both in biblical times and today. Life gets messy, even in the church. Maybe *especially* in the church.

It's easier to ignore these hard details, isn't it? But we are about to dive right in.

Although the custom of the day was for men to have concubines and many wives, forcibly taking a woman was never okay with God. It was sin. It always has been and always will be. Yes, even for the very important man of God, Abraham. He didn't get a hall pass for this one just for being a big shot, Bible-time celebrity.

God wasn't pleased with what Abraham did and you can bet your britches Abraham knew better. Abraham was a man of God after all. Because his actions went against God's design for sex and marriage, we can be certain that the whole ordeal didn't feel right in anyone's soul. Sin never does. Even if it is what everyone else is doing.

The actions of men towards women in the Word of God are in no way a reflection of *God's* personal view of women. If we don't understand that, we may be tempted to walk away from a God who we incorrectly perceive views women as objects to be abused. That's not God's heart at all. Don't confuse the mindset of men towards women with the heart of *God* toward women. If they were the same, I'd beat you to the exit door on this Christian faith thing. Period. I'd never follow a God who views women the way men back then did, the way that, sadly, some Christian men still do today.

Women of the Bible had the same feelings and emotions we

do. They are characters in the Bible, but they are not fictional. They suffered, laughed, rejoiced, and cried just like we do today. They dealt with PMS, hormones, menopause, and meltdowns. They had dreams and goals. They faced stress and grief. They cared about their kids and worried about the future. There were days they didn't have a clue what to make for dinner. They got headaches and toothaches. They struggled with insecurity and chin hairs, with stretch marks and sagging chests.

Hagar would have been horrified and traumatized over the whole ordeal like you or I'd be today. First of all, Hagar would have wanted to be the first wife, the chosen wife. Hagar didn't have the privilege of dreaming of a wedding or saying *yes* to a dress. No little girl grows up dreaming of being sold as a slave. While Sarah was the wanted, chosen one, Hagar was someone's property.

Sarah's life wasn't perfect, either. Do you remember when Abraham lied by saying Sarah was his sister, instead of telling the truth that she was his wife? Because he feared for his life he let men haul his wife off to be violated. Thankfully, God stepped in sparing Sarah from any harm. But Abraham abandoned his role as protector and he abandoned his commitment to his wife. He let men take his wife away, he knew she would face indescribable horror, but saving his own neck was more important to him. He failed her in the most terrible way imaginable. Genesis 20 tells the full story.

Okay, I need a break. I will go reheat my coffee (for the thirteenth time), devour some dark chocolate, and be right back.

It's all so troubling, isn't it? Not the part about me reheating the same cup of coffee. The part about Abraham violating a slave and not protecting his wife.

This chapter does have a positive ending, I promise. I've learned the hard way that I can't get victory over things I refuse to process honestly. I'm taking deep breaths as I type. How are you doing? Stay with me.

AMY JOY STOUT

I have never suffered this sort of abuse, but so many women today and throughout history have. Abuse by godly men is very real for so many women. We owe it to those women to be open about what they have endured. (If you have been sexually assaulted, my heart hurts for you. So does God's. I pray you have supportive people in your life who can walk with you on this journey to healing. You're worth counseling. You deserve healing. Whatever it takes, and as long as it takes, you're worth it.)

My heart wrestles with God because He honors Abraham. There are even Sunday School songs about him. Why does God bless people who hurt us? Those people who make foolish decisions that cause great pain for others to endure. God elevates Abraham, praises him, and even gives him serious ink in His Word. No rebuke, no discipline, no caveats or even a clarifying fine print somewhere at the bottom of the page explaining how God *really* feels about what Abraham did and how He really feels about women. Nope, God just says Abraham is the Father of Faith. I'm suddenly feeling the need for a hot bubble bath. I take those when I'm stressed and need an escape—just ask my kids.

Since we are here, I might as well keep going; it's kind of like when I'm at the dentist getting cavities filled. Just do them all. I'd rather not come back to do this again.

So then there's David. He is acclaimed as a man after God's own heart. And guess what? He too took a woman (2 Samuel 11). He saw Bathsheba and wanted her. So he told his servants to get her. We have no idea how violent that whole process was. But we know he had power and she did not.

Bathsheba had been bathing on a rooftop, and in case you think Bathsheba is at fault, I will remind you that that was as normal as showering in our indoor bathrooms is today. It's what everyone did. Bathing on a roof wasn't what scandalous women did who wanted to seduce men.

94

The only home with a view would have been David's palace, since it towered above every other structure. He had the only view in town and something tells me this wasn't his first time he found himself enjoying it. David took Bathsheba, impregnated her, and then murdered her husband in cold blood.

How can God say David was a man after his own heart? Frankly, it hurts my soul to read those words. Did Bathsheba's life not matter? Under what carpet does this get swept? I found a few good deals on shaggy carpets online if you're looking for one to help hide these hard-to-digest pages. The Lord knows that's precisely what many of us Christians do. We shove it under a thick rug and pretend it isn't there until so much piles up that we stop engaging with God at all. Because none of this seems okay. And what on earth do you do with your relationship with God when this is the way women are treated in the book He wrote for us to read? What did He think we were supposed to make of it all?

Things get even more horrifying as God punishes David by making the women in his household endure more sexual abuse (2 Samuel 12:11-12). It's more than my heart can bear. I can't even handle typing up a summary of it, so I will spare us the details.

Then we read in Psalm 51 that David says, "Only against God have I sinned." Um, excuse me? No, David, you created unimaginable horror, grief, loss, and brokenness almost everywhere you went. You can start with funerals and gravesites. How about the mother who lost her son, the children who lost their daddy, the woman who lost her husband? How about the woman who was downright terrified when she got summoned to you? Are you sure you can't think of *anyone* you have wronged, besides God?

I'm about to shut my windows to scream. If you care to join me, feel free. This stresses me out to my very core and makes me want to devour a big bowl of restaurant style tortilla chips and homemade pico all by myself. The good chips, not the generic kind–not for this. Maybe you understand. About both the chip-eating and the Bible-processing. I'm so glad to know I'm not alone. Yes, I know I need to deal with my food cravings. Thank you for the reminder.

One more hard one, okay? It's about Abraham's nephew. Warning: It's a *Lot* to process. (Sorry . . . that was corny. I get awkward when I'm stressed.)

Here we go: Lot offered his daughters to sex-crazy men so they could rape them (Genesis 19:5-8). God doesn't punish Lot for this, though. Instead, He punishes Lot's *wife* by turning her into a pillar of salt for looking back as they are running away from their burning home.

Who wouldn't turn back to look? It seems like a natural response. A reflex, really. I would be thinking: "My town is engulfed in a violent inferno. I can feel the heat at my back. I can see the flames' reflection raging in the night sky; ashes rain down covering my clothes like fresh snow. Our home is engulfed. But don't look? Riiiiiiight. Sure thing. Roger that."

Lot's wife transforms into a pillar of salt and yet Lot can offer his daughters to sex traffickers and not even get so much as a teeny tiny time-out?

How is this fair?

It makes me feel like God doesn't value His daughters. These stories make zero sense to me. I'd have been a pillar of salt right next to Lot's wife if I was there. You might as well pass the pepper, people.

I don't have the answers. No one does. Scholars try, but I'm not sure why. (I didn't intend for that to rhyme but you don't mind if we roll with it, do you? Cuz I'm too worked up to rewrite this chapter. Thanks. You're the best.)

People try to spiritualize this. However, this non-seminary attending, ordinary woman right here knows there are some things we can't spiritualize away no matter how much we wish we could. I want scholars and pastors to say, even if just once, "I have no idea what these men were thinking. This is stupid. What they did was horrible. That's all I got on this awful, good-for-nothing mess. It's inexcusable and unacceptable."

———

So there it is.

We went *there* and talked about it. We got real. God can handle our honestly, so I think we can too.

Now what? Where do we go from here?

I have spent many years, taking long walks with God while pouring my heart out to Him about these specific stories. For the most part, God has not answered me. Through the years though I believe he slowly whispered a few truths to me. These truths are the foundation from which I must build my view or I don't stand a chance of hanging in there with God through this. The first one is this:

*God does not owe me answers.*

Before you write me off because this seems unfair, hear me out. He doesn't owe me answers (read the book of Job if you're not convinced). I have gotten to the place where I really am okay with not having answers. I don't say that flippantly and I'm not speaking from the cheap seats. I have learned, through an exhausting yet beautiful wrestling match with God, to trust Him with my questions and I believe He trusts me *back*. He trusts that I won't quit seeking Him, even when I'm downright mad at Him. I have surrendered. He is bigger than me. So are His ways and His thoughts. There are a great host of things I will never understand.

He has my heart even still. He has won my affection for keeps. He earned my trust for good–like forever and always no matter what. He's got all of me.

He knows that I'm going to keep bringing the tough questions. I will still cry out in my hurt, confusion, and disappointment over the crazy nonsense of some of the stories in His Word. But there's no doubt that He knows He's got me and my heart even still. I don't always like the decisions He makes. But I do like Him–a lot. I like Him and He likes me. I know He values His daughters even if earthly men have not.

Here's the second thing I've learned through these hard stories:

*I am David and I am Abraham.*

(I'm not confused about my gender, though, just so we're clear.)

I'm just like David and Abraham. I've hurt people. I've used people for my own gain. I've taken what I wanted while disregarding the effects on real heart-pumping, oxygen-breathing people, many of whom are the ones I love and care about the most in this world.

I made a mess of things more times than I care to count. A filthy, muddy, rainy day mess.

Yet, God *still* calls me His beloved. He still says, "Amy Joy Stout has a heart for me. She loves me. She believes in me. She has faith." This brings tears to my eyes. How would the people I have wounded feel if they heard God say, "Amy loves me," when I failed to show them love? How do they make sense of that?

That's the same thing God did for the Father of our Faith Abraham and King David. He looked past the junk in their hearts. He saw the good. He saw who else they were. He didn't define them by their mess-ups. He knew who they could be and who they would turn out to be. He saw their potential and their purpose. Instead of bringing up their baggage, He brought up their bright spots.

God is so good like that. He is so wise like that. So forgiving like that. So gracious like that. That's how and why I can keep walking towards Him, with Him. Because He has treated me with the same kindness and mercy that He extended to the men I'm frustrated with. Others have been frustrated with me too.

Here's the third, and probably most important, truth I believe through all this mess.

*I will go on with God.*

I have never been physically violated, but I do feel the pain of Sarah, Hagar, and Bathsheba. It's still hard stuff for me to read no matter how many times I read it. Yet, I *still* read God's Word daily. I still hunger and thirst for it like my next breath depends on it. Because it does.

My flesh tells me to dig my high heels into the ground. (It's gotta be heels otherwise my jeans will drag on the floor. I'm too tall for petite, too short for regular. The struggle is real.) When the Word is painful to read, I feel like quitting. When God seems cruel, harsh, and unloving, when bullies go unpunished and women go unprotected, I want to shut the Bible and just pretend it's not real. But it was very real.

These are the seasons of wrestling with God.

But through these seasons, this is where I decide: Will I keep walking with God or without Him? I have two options and I will make a choice. *Bitter or sweet, Amy. Which way will you go?*

I can stay on the road with God without the answers, or go on without Him and without the answers. The way I see it, I won't have all the answers either way. Either way things won't always make sense. That's just how our human existence goes.

I don't stand a chance in this harsh world without my Jesus. So I choose to go on with Him without answers.

*God, if you don't explain yourself, I'm still journeying on with you.*

*If I don't understand your ways, I will still seek you with all of my heart and the best of my intentions.*

*If I don't approve of all the stories in the Bible, I will still love Your Word.*

*If I'm disappointed, I will declare that you know what you're doing, because you know things I don't and see things I can't.*

*I recognize, Jesus, that you came to earth and changed the way women were treated. You changed the value system for females. You stood up for us. You defended us. You protected us. You cared for us. You invited us to join your life and your ministry. You set us free. You were a man who treated women with dignity, kindness and respect. You changed our world. I choose to see your heart for us.*

*If you bless someone who hurt me, you don't owe me an explanation.*

*If you declare that someone loves you even if they have not been loving towards me, that's cool too.*

*I trust you.*

*I believe you trust me too.*

And off we go, together still . . .

———

**Choosing Sweetness: Going Deeper with God**

> *For my thoughts are not your thoughts, neither are your ways my ways declares the Lord. As the heavens are higher than the earth, so are my ways higher than your ways and my thoughts higher than your thoughts.*

> — ISAIAH 55:8-9

> *Who is this that darkens my counsel with words without knowledge. Brace yourself like a man and I will question you and you will answer me. Where were you when I laid the earth's foundation . . . .*

> — JOB 38:2-4

- Consider reading Job Chapters 38-40.
- Do you have hard to read places in the Bible? Why are they hard? Does that impact your view of or relationship with God? Can you go on with God without the answers?
- Do you trust God and can He trust you? Why or why not?

---

SWEET NUGGETS: TAKEAWAYS TO REMEMBER

*Actions of men toward women in the Word of God do not reflect God's personal view of women.*

*I trust God with my cringing heart and my agonizing mind. He trusts me back.*

*I don't always like God's decisions but I sure do like Him.*

*Instead of bringing up our baggage, God focuses on our bright spots.*

*I choose to go on with God, even without all the answers.*

# 9

## SET HER FREE

*M*y husband worked for the maintenance department of a college when we were first married. He would spend eight straight hours mowing the 100+ acres of lawn that made up the campus.

I'd often ask him what he thought about while he sat on that tractor. He had hours upon hours to daydream, solve problems, and have make believe conversations with himself. So much could have been happening inside that balding head of his.

Every time I would ask him, his answer was usually the same: "Nothing."

"Nothing? Really?!"

"I thought about mowing the grass in a straight line. That's what I thought about—the grass."

How. Can. That. Be. Possible!

That sounds like a vacation—a vacation from myself. Oh, pretty please, can I go there? Someone, please, book me a flight to destination "Think Nothing" for one week. I don't care how much it costs.

My mind doesn't leave my mind alone—ever. Can you relate?

There is a woman in the Bible who I'm sure felt the same way. You may know her. Her name was Martha. You likely think of her as the woman who was too busy, anxious, and worried to worship Jesus. She's often beat down over the fact that she was serving Jesus in the kitchen rather than sitting at Jesus' feet like her sister Mary. We praise Mary but we condemn Martha. Mary hears, "You're amazing!" while Martha hears, "What's the matter with you?"

We've been repeatedly instructed to emulate Mary while steering clear of Martha's behavior. For the life of me I can't figure out why. I feel like she has been unfairly judged and misunderstood for generations.

Let's take a look at their story:

> As Jesus and his disciples were on their way, He came to a village where a woman named Martha opened her home to him. She had a sister called Mary, who sat at the Lord's feet listening to what He said. But Martha was distracted by all the preparations that had to be made. She came to Him and asked, "Lord, don't you care that my sister has left me to do the work by myself? Tell her to help me!" "Martha, Martha," the Lord answered, "You are worried and upset about many things, but only one thing is needed. Mary has chosen what is better, and it will not be taken from her."
>
> — LUKE 10:38 - 42

My husband has begged me to write about Martha for years. I think he's tired of hearing me talk about it. We were at a conference once when the speaker used Martha as a negative example and Cory squeezed my hand, leaned over, and said, "Would you please write that book?" A few months later, he was reading a book on theology and there it was again: Martha-bashing. My husband turned to me again, "Write the book!"

I can't help wanting to come to her defense. I'd really love to clear her name by rewriting her legacy. I know I don't have that kind of influence but I *do* have a glimmer of hope that by honoring her in this chapter we may begin to think differently not only about Martha but also others around us who we have judged perhaps a little too harshly.

Do you think there's even the slightest of possibilities that we have misunderstood the people we think poorly of? That maybe we don't have the *whole* story? God may ask us to give those people a break after all these years, and finally let them off the hook we stuck them on too.

Wouldn't it be the biggest bonus if, as we do that for other people, we end up doing the same for ourselves? After all, a woman who harshly critiques others, harshly critiques herself. We are incapable of extending grace to anyone else if we won't extend grace to ourselves first.

I know what you're thinking. "But Jesus said that Mary has 'chosen what is better'!" Yes, He did. Worship over works is an important principle and we will get to that in a minute. But what about the following, equally as important concept? *God made Martha to be Martha and God made Mary to be Mary.* Just like God made me to be me and you to be you, He doesn't want us to be anyone else.

Take a look again at the scripture above. What did Martha do? Before she started the preparations? What happened first?

Martha *welcomed* Jesus into her home.

There is no other place in scripture where we are told that anyone opened their home to Jesus in *this* way. A Pharisee invited Jesus over for a meal (likely with ulterior motives) and Zacchaeus welcomed Jesus into his home only *after* Jesus invited himself. No one else welcomed Jesus the way Martha did.

She opened her home to him. Because Martha invited Jesus, Mary got to sit with Jesus. Mary has Martha to thank for that.

Keep in mind that in a time before cell phones and email, Martha didn't even know that Jesus and His disciples were coming! No warning, no time to prepare, and no Chick-fil-A drive through (and it was Sunday anyway, right?). She didn't have a microwave, no access to a modern grocery store, no pizza delivery.

Are you picturing this with me, ladies? I'm panicking just thinking about it. She had thirteen grown, tired, dirty, and hungry men to feed and house for the night. Because of the time this took place in Jesus's ministry, it's safe to conclude he had all twelve disciples with Him.

She welcomed them.

Why isn't Martha remembered as the "Woman Who Welcomed Jesus into Her Home"? It seems entirely reasonable to remember her this way, don't you think? Why isn't *that* what everyone thinks of when her name is mentioned?

It reminds me of how, sometimes, all people seem to remember is the one time when you blew it. No matter what else you have done right, you're forever misunderstood and misjudged. Martha knew the feeling. Martha has endured many insults from pulpits and stages around the world. But the truth of the matter is that Martha was a woman who wanted to be with Jesus. She wasn't too busy for Jesus. Why on earth would she have invited Jesus into her home otherwise? *Too busy, my foot.*

Martha dropped everything she had going on that day to welcome Him into her home without warning. I can't tell you how many opportunities I have missed to host guests. I usually take a quick mental inventory of my home, decide that I have nothing to serve and that my house is too messy, and decline to extend an invitation.

Not our girl Martha. Ready or not, she wanted Jesus there.

To me, this is *beautiful*. To me, this is true worship. To me, this is what we should remember her for. I want to be like Martha. When my tired feet hit the floor in the morning, I want to welcome Jesus into my space. Whatever the mess, whatever my lack, whatever I perceive hinders me from true intimacy with my Jesus and whatever else I have going on that day, I want to do what Martha did . . . open my home, my life and my schedule to Him.

"But Martha was distracted by all the preparations that had to be made . . . . " Did you catch six very important yet often overlooked words in that text? *Preparations that had to be made.* When you have thirteen men to feed and no take out options, those are the facts, people. Someone had to make preparations. These men were hungry. Don't over-spiritualize these moments in Martha's home. They unfolded like they would if *you* had thirteen unexpected guests show up for dinner. And I believe Jesus was looking forward to a delicious, satisfying meal from a capable cook. He was, keep in mind, fully man!

I had a Martha moment once when hosting twenty-four relatives in my home over Christmas for three days. Ten adults and fourteen kids under the age of twelve in my home for three days. *I hosted twenty-four people in my home for three days.* I felt the need to repeat myself in case you missed the gravity of what I said. That means morning, noon, and night for three days in a row, 24/7. Get it? Oh, and let me throw this little detail in there: this was my husband's family. (Now some of you are really feeling me.) I thought this was a nice daughter-in-law thing to do. No, it's a *dumb* daughter-in-law thing to do. We do get along and everyone loves each other—usually. (Peace at all costs is the name of the game . . . moving along . . . . )

While everyone relaxed, I was hostessing. Preparations had to be made. The food, the dishes, the cleanup. The food. The cleanup. The food. The cleanup. Oh sorry, I was having a flashback panic attack. *It's over, Amy. Breathe.* People needed things non-stop: a band aid, an extra pillow, toys, snacks, toilet paper, Advil . . . . (that last one was for me). Someone is hungry, something is broken, someone is bored. On and on it went.

My mother-in-law said that was her favorite Christmas ever. I understand why. For once, she didn't have to be Martha. She got to be Mary that Christmas. She deserved it. If anyone deserved a break, it's my amazing mother-in-law. For the record, that wasn't my favorite Christmas. Also, for the record, we have not hosted the family Christmas since. I'm still recovering a decade later. My husband recently volunteered us to host his parents fiftieth wedding anniversary without asking me. But we won't talk about that right now.

I honestly think Jesus was thrilled that Martha was in the kitchen making preparations. He was smelling the aroma of a hearty dinner and looking forward to a nourishing meal in the company of friends. See, Martha's time sitting with Jesus was coming soon: she would sit with Him at her table as they shared a meal together. It was coming!

In those moments I truly believe Martha was right where she should have been, doing exactly what she was doing. Martha was serving Jesus by meeting His physical needs of shelter and nourishment. God *gave* Martha the gift of hospitality. Jesus was disciplining Martha for her attitude, not for her actions. It's where she was in her heart, not where she was in her home, that got her in trouble.

Mary became a distraction to Martha. Martha compared herself to her free as a bird sister, and in so doing a critical, complaining spirit took over. A discontented heart soon followed. It always does. It's so easy to judge the actions of the women around us. We typically want others around us on our band wagon, passionate about what we are passionate about, involved with what we deem important. We want everyone else doing what we'd like them to do. It sure is easy to get frustrated when no one is helping us with the thing we care so much about.

Martha looked up from her place of responsibility, saw Mary resting and probably thought: "Are you kidding me right now? Isn't that just precious. Hellooooo. Hello?! If you would help me out with my burden for a moment, then maybe I could actually join you and do nothing but sit there soaking it all in along with you! Why won't you help me?"

God made Martha to be Martha. God made Mary to be Mary. It's simple, yet profound. He made them different because He wanted to. He liked them both. He was pleased with who they both were. Neither of them were supposed to be like the other and—for crying out loud—nor were they supposed to do what the other was doing. God never implied that, yet somehow we do.

God gave Martha her hospitality gift. You can be sure He was glad He did. He was on the receiving end of the very gift He assigned to her. God gave Mary her tender spirit. He knew she thrived on relationships, reflection, and conversation. He liked them both. He loved them both. He made them the way He did *on purpose*.

So when Martha started whining about her sister, Jesus wasn't going to have it. Jesus told Martha only one thing is needed and that Mary had chosen what was better and it wouldn't be taken from her. Jesus was defending Mary like a father breaks up a sibling rivalry. God won't tolerate His kids picking on each other. He won't take sides, either. Martha's attitude needed to change, but her actions and the way she welcomed Jesus into her home were very good. Admirable, even. Let's not lose sight of that.

I'm pretty sure that *one thing* Jesus was talking about was the one thing He said was the greatest commandment of all: Love me with all of your heart, soul, mind and strength. In that moment in the kitchen Martha lost sight of that *one thing*. But

I'm confident Jesus was still happy she was doing *her thing* right there in the kitchen.

I'd love the luxury of sitting with Jesus in His Word all day. That sounds divine, right? But God nudges me out of my cozy chair and gently but firmly says, "I know you'd rather linger longer, but there are preparations to be made today that only you can do." My work is worship when done with the right heart—a heart that's focused on Jesus.

God made you on purpose and He wants you to be free to be yourself. He wants you to love Him well out of an overflow of who *you* are, not who someone else is. He likes you. And yes, He even likes the women you don't. *Ouch.*

Jesus loved Martha exactly as she was and appreciated her gifts. He admonished her attitude in this one situation. But the bottom line is, Martha was still the woman who welcomed Jesus into her home. Martha wasn't supposed to be like her sister. I don't think that was the point of Jesus' rebuke—not at all. But she was supposed to be herself well. We all are.

We are going to keep talking about Martha and Mary for one more chapter. My favorite part of their story is still coming.

But for now let's set Martha free from our unfair judgment. Can we do that? She made one mistake. Can we choose not to define her by something we don't fully understand? Is there another woman in your real life that you have written off? Assigned a poor reputation to? She blew it once and now you have her pegged? Would you consider rewriting her legacy? Would you even consider defending her when people put her down?

Martha was one amazing woman who has taught me so much. She is the only recorded woman in the Bible who welcomed Jesus into her home.

How cool is that?

---

## CHOOSING SWEETNESS: GOING DEEPER WITH GOD

*A wife of noble character . . . sets about her work
vigorously; her arms are strong for her tasks.*

— PROVERBS 31:1-17

*A good name is more desirable than great riches; to be
esteemed is better than silver or gold.*

— PROVERBS 22:1

*Above all, love each other deeply, because love covers
over a multitude of sins. Offer hospitality to one
another without grumbling. Each one should use
whatever gift he has received to serve others . . . .*

— 1 PETER 4:8-10

- What do you appreciate about Martha? Would you consider thinking differently about her reputation?
- Do you feel misunderstood? Is there someone else who you may be judging unfairly?
- Do you easily get distracted by other women? Do you project your own passions, personality, callings, gifting, or capacity on them?
- Do you feel pressure to be like anyone else? Do you believe God is calling you to be free to be yourself but to be her well?

## SWEET NUGGETS: TAKEAWAYS TO REMEMBER

*A woman who harshly critiques other women first harshly critiques herself. We can't extend grace to others if we won't extend grace to ourselves.*

*Comparison leads to a critical spirit which is followed by a discontented heart.*

*God was disciplining Martha for where she was in her heart, not for where she was in her home.*

*Jesus won't tolerate his girls picking on one another. He won't take sides.*

*God made you to be you on purpose. Be her well.*

## LOVE HIM LIKE HE MADE YOU TO

*J* don't have a sister. The older I get the harder not having one becomes. While growing up, I didn't mind one bit that I was my daddy's only special little girl and I never had to share a room—that was the best. But now, I long for a sister more than ever. I'm so grateful that my daughters have each other. Every once in a while I have to remind them of what a blessing it is to have a sister.

As precious as it is, I do know the sister relationship can also be delicate. It certainly was for Mary and Martha.

There are a couple more nuggets I want us to glean from these sisters before we move on. Is that okay if we spend one more chapter with the Woman Who Welcomed Jesus into Her Home? I believe you'll be glad we did.

Grab your Bible and read John 11:1-21. The Word is alive and God rejoices so much when we read it. Here are two excerpts from the passage in case you're all snuggled in your favorite chair. (And in which case, you're not moving for nothing, are you? It's okay, I gotcha.)

*Now a man named Lazarus was sick. He was from*

*Bethany, the village of Mary and her sister Martha. (This Mary, whose brother Lazarus now lay sick, was the same one who poured perfume on the Lord and wiped His feet with her hair.) So the sisters sent word to Jesus, "Lord, the one you love is sick." When He heard this, Jesus said, "This sickness will not end in death. No, it's for God's glory so that God's Son may be glorified through it." Now Jesus loved Martha and her sister and Lazarus. So when He heard that Lazarus was sick, He stayed where He was two more days, and then He said to his disciples, "Let us go back to Judea . . . . " On His arrival, Jesus found that Lazarus had already been in the tomb for four days. Now, Bethany was less than two miles from Jerusalem, and many Jews had come to Martha and Mary to comfort them in the loss of their brother. When Martha heard that Jesus was coming, she went out to meet Him, but Mary stayed at home. "Lord," Martha said to Jesus, "If you had been here, my brother would not have died."*

I love seeing glimpses of Mary and Martha's personalities here. What were the two sisters doing? Mary was engaging with the people visiting them in their home to pay their condolences. Of course she was. She stayed home to be with people. Mary found great comfort in their company.

What about Martha? What was she up to? The second she hears that Jesus is on His way, she bolts out the door. She leaves the guests, and I don't think she thought twice about their feelings on it, either. She was after Jesus. She had to get to Him. She was willing to leave the comfort of the crowd to get to the One and Only.

Can you tell that Martha is a go-getter? She's a bold, determined, and capable woman. Mary is reflective and likely a more thorough decision-maker. She's probably the more sensitive of the two, as well.

Lazarus had died and Jesus was late. And yet, what Martha did, in the midst of her pain and disappointment in Jesus was remarkable. She resolved to get to Jesus. She made her way through the streets, craning her neck, squinting her eyes, scanning the crowd for Him. She searched for Him like she meant it. This was no lip service going through the motions, not really engaged, kind of search. No, she was all in.

With every fiber of my being, I want to do what our girl Martha had the maturity to do. Finding Jesus meant something to this girl. She longed for Him even when He had severely disappointed her. If He had only been there, her brother would not have died. That's a pretty serious allegation.

*"Lord," Martha said to Jesus, "if you had been here my brother would not have died. But I know that even now God will give you whatever you ask."*

— JOHN 11:21

I don't know if you have any "Jesus, but even now" situations in your life, but I know I do. Situations that seem long dead in my family, in my marriage, in our ministry. Places where I feel hopeless. I want to have the kind of faith Martha had. I want to believe that even though something seems dead, *even now*, God can revive it. I want the kind of passion and energy it takes to make my way to God even though all hope seems lost. Even though He hasn't come through for me yet. Even though the lights went out and the seats emptied out a very long time ago. *God, but even now.*

I told you Martha was an amazing woman.

Has your heart been hurt too? Has God disappointed you by

not showing up when you wanted Him to? Does it seem like He stood you up? Was He too late?

Don't resign. Don't quit. As I type these words, I type them for myself as much as I do for you. *Amy, for crying out loud, please resist the urge to sit and sulk over this. Get up, get after God, He has yet to move in your situation but girl, He still can.*

With no sign of hope Martha got up, wiped her tears, found her purse, and bolted for the door. She carried the same pain she had carried the last four days. Yet, her hope was still Jesus. Remarkable. It's tempting to wait for the one who let us down to make the next move isn't it? It would have been understandable had Martha sat in her house with a chip on her shoulder waiting for Jesus to come to *her*. He was the late one after all. *He* let *her* down. She doesn't take the victim mindset. She doesn't dig her high heels in the dirt while waiting for God to show up to her. No, she acts like the big girl she is. She makes the next move. She makes her way to Jesus. She is strong. She is mature. She is *grown up*. She is *beautiful*.

Instead of sulking, she runs to Him. And this was even after the verbal spanking she received from Jesus when He was in her home, as we discussed in the last chapter. She didn't let that one embarrassing episode ruin her relationship with Jesus. She accepted the rebuke and kept going. She was teachable. She didn't ditch the one who disciplined her. That's not an easy thing to do.

*Draw near to God and He will draw near to you.*

— JAMES 4:8

*You will seek me and find me when you seek me with
all of your heart. I will be found by you, declares the
Lord.*

— JEREMIAH 29:13-14

There is just one more thing I really want you to see. It's just
one of the sweetest stories in the Bible. See if you agree.

*Six days before the Passover, Jesus came to Bethany,
where Lazarus lived, whom Jesus had raised from
the dead. Here a dinner was given in Jesus' honor.
Martha served, while Lazarus was among those
reclining at the table with him. Then Mary took
about a pint of pure nard, an expensive perfume;
she poured it on Jesus' feet and wiped his feet with
her hair. And the house was filled with the
fragrance of the perfume.*

— JOHN 12:1-3

Mary usually gets all the glory from this passage—rightfully
so. She deserves to be honored for what she did.

But did you catch something else in these verses? There are
two important words in the second verse that are often
overlooked.

*Martha served.*

I can't tell you how much this delights me. Martha blew it
once but she didn't let one mistake stop her. She didn't throw in
the towel or quit because of shame. She didn't let a setback
derail her from her calling. She didn't allow a little drama to get
in the way. It seems nothing could convince her to stop being
who God made her to be or to stop doing what God made her
to do.

116

She was back at it! She didn't let Jesus' rebuke crush her spirit or discourage her from using her gifts again. Atta girl, Martha!

Martha was a strong woman. A woman with a sound mind. She was a woman who was *growing up* right along with growing old. She wasn't letting life make her *ugly*. She was emerging *beautiful* through it all. I love this so very much.

God liked them both, Mary and Martha. He did. He made them different on purpose. He prefers it that way! You don't need to be anyone else but you! We are free to be ourselves. We don't need to change who we are. However, we do need to be committed to growing, learning, and maturing so that we can do more than just be ourselves. So that we can be ourselves *well.*

God doesn't compare you to any other woman and He doesn't want you to be any other woman. He doesn't want you to be Mary. He doesn't want you to be Martha. He wants you to be you. Okay?

It's time to set yourself free. While you're at it, set the women around you free too. We'll all breathe a collective sigh of relief if you do.

We don't know how that evening unfolded after Mary poured perfume on Jesus' feet. Oh, how I wish we did. As I close this chapter, I want to express what I imagine happened. After all the guests went home and only the two sisters remained, perhaps the conversation went something like this:

Martha (while doing the dishes, of course):

"Mary, I saw what you did tonight. That was beautiful. The aroma from the perfume you poured over Jesus saturated the air with such tenderness and love. I saw the look on Jesus's face. Mary, he was touched by you. He was overwhelmed by the depth of your expression of worship to him. He understood your sacrifice. He delighted in your bold display of love. You blessed Him deeply, Mary. I couldn't have done what you did...I don't think I have it in me to be expressive in that way. It would have been so awkward had I tried. But watching you love Him in that way? It was beautiful and profound. I'm so proud to be your sister."

Mary (while helping Martha clean up . . . *please* tell me she helped):

"Martha, I saw what you did tonight. I saw what you did all week in preparation for this. The dinner you prepared was delicious. It was perfect. I saw Jesus's face when you served Him his meal. He was so excited. His eyes lit up. I saw Him give you that gentle wink of approval. The meal smelled as good as it tasted. I saw the love and gratitude in His eyes for you. You ministered deeply to Jesus tonight, Martha. You did. You nourished the Son of God. You fed our Messiah. He was deeply grateful for the expression of love and devotion you displayed to him tonight. I couldn't have done what you did . . . I wouldn't know where to begin. It would have ended up a culinary disaster. Jesus would have gone hungry, that's for sure. But watching you do your thing, I'm just so proud of you, Martha."

Sweet friend, be yourself well.

Love God like He made you to.

---

**Choosing Sweetness: Going Deeper with God**

*I praise you because I am fearfully and wonderfully made.*

— PSALM 139:14

*All the days ordained for me were written before one of them came to be.*

— PSALM 139:16

*See, I have engraved you on the palm of my hand. Your walls are ever before me.*

— ISAIAH 49:16

*He will take great delight in you . . . .*

— ZEPHANIAH 3:17

*He who touches you touches the apple of his eye.*

— ZECHARIAH 2:8

- How has God uniquely created you to love Him?
- Are there any women who God is asking you to set free? To redefine? To let off the hook?
- Can you celebrate the way God made other women?
- If you had a season of rebuke, did that sideline you or are you back at it doing what God made you to do?
- Are you teachable and responsive? Do you have courage and resolve to not throw in the towel over one episode?
- Have you been embarrassed over a public mistake? Can you make a decision to get over it rather than hiding in shame?

———

SWEET NUGGETS: TAKEAWAYS TO REMEMBER

*Even though something seems dead, God can still revive it.*

*He may have yet to move in your situation but, girl, He still can.*

*Run to Him.*

*Accept the rebuke and keep going. Don't allow a mistake to convince you to stop being who God made you to be.*

*Love God out of the overflow of how He made you.*

*Be yourself well.*

# 11

## DAILY DOSES

*I*t was our first family vacation.

It took us two years but somehow we managed to scrape together enough money for round trip plane tickets from Minneapolis to Denver. We were headed to a log cabin in the mountains of Durango, Colorado. Our son was sixteen months old and I was three months pregnant.

We anticipated hiking rugged mountain trials, relaxing alongside rushing streams, soaking in the crisp, fresh mountain air, strolling through quaint towns, eating yummy treats purchased from an old-time ice cream parlor, and delighting in the surprise of seeing the occasional forest critter, all while our son nestled contently in his toddler backpack that we scored at a thrift store for next to nothing. We couldn't wait.

Our little boy did fantastically on his first flight. A few books, a container of Cheerios, and his stuffed Veggie Tales friend was all he needed to be entertained for hours. Life was good. Ministry was good. We were happy—finally. I had that glow and relished the fact that *this* was what "adult-ing" was supposed to look like for us. Finally. Life was right. We needed right for a change.

But *right* was about to bail on us.

After an uneventful flight, we exited the plane and headed to the rental car counter. This is where things began to take a turn.

Since we weren't yet twenty-five years old at the time, we were casually informed that we couldn't rent the car we had already reserved and paid for.

It was 10:00 p.m. We were out of cheerios. Bob the Tomato wasn't cutting it anymore. A toddler meltdown loomed ahead. I envisioned us homeless, helpless, stranded like vagabonds in the airport for a week until our return flight. A sad, helpless, young family living out of suitcases begging real grown-ups for cold chicken nuggets leftover from their kids' not-so-happy meal.

My heart rate increased and my body tensed up as I tried to comfort my now exhausted sixteen-month old son. We were all tired. We wanted the keys to the car we booked so we could get out of the airport and on to our long-awaited vacation.

Neither of those things would be happening anytime soon.

Mr. Are You Even Out of High School Car Rental Dude wasn't going to budge. I felt like grabbing this young kid by his clip-on bow tie, pulling him up and over the counter inches from my face and saying, "Look, kid. Here's the deal. You have ten seconds to produce keys. Any keys. I don't care if they are your keys, your boss's keys, your girlfriend's keys, the janitor's keys, or your mama's keys. Somebody is going to cough up wheels. Like, now. Please and thank you."

Instead, I looked at the cold filthy cement floor beneath me, slumped down in resignation with Drew in my arms and thought, *this is it.* Our vacation would be spent slouched under the counter of Alamo at the Denver airport.

My husband was handling it, calmly talking through the situation, but sitting there on the floor with my toddler, it didn't appear to me that calm was working. Remember, my husband is the kind, rational, non-demanding, always-in-control-of-his-emotions-and-tone peacemaker type. Like I said before: oversaved.

Me? Well, I'm Italian. Enough said.

I regained my strength, stood up, and respectfully asked for the manager. This pregnant mama bear had had enough. The manager made his less than enthusiastic appearance from behind the wall where I knew he overheard the entire conversation. He looked at me like I was pathetic. Clearly he wasn't a parent. And clearly I *was* pathetic.

His eyes were heavy and bored. His voice monotone. He wasn't at all passionate about his job, that much was clear. He told us we could rent the car if we paid an extra fee for being under twenty-five. Seriously? We could have solved this ordeal more than thirty minutes ago.

We got the keys and gathered our things so that we could get going as quickly as possible.

But then I felt myself begin to bleed.

We frantically found an airport payphone and called my doctor with a plastic calling card that had twelve minutes left on it. (This was life pre-cell phones.) My doctor told me to lay low and rest. Ah, Doc? Did you catch the "we're in Colorado on vacation" part of this conversation? We have plans, none of which involve "laying low."

As we drove the six hours along windy mountain roads, we didn't talk much. We prayed silently with heaviness in our hearts too afraid to utter out loud what we both were thinking. If we didn't say it maybe it wouldn't really be happening. We could pretend it wasn't happening. Vacations are supposed to be a happy escape from real life. We tried hard to escape the real life unfolding in those very quiet hours on our way to the vacation we were now beginning to dread.

We checked into our cabin with unease at what would take place in this strange place far away from home. Our return flight was in one week. I wanted my own home so badly. I wanted my doctor and my friends. I wanted my mom. We entered the beautiful log cabin with its breathtaking view. Windows let light in from floor to ceiling, but despair hung like musty, heavy drapes over the beauty they framed. It felt dark in that well-lit cabin.

The towels were white. The sheets were white. We needed our damage deposit back. I wasn't sure how I was going to bright-red-bleed my baby right out of me without doing permanent damage to those white linens. There was a mess in my soul and a mess coming out of me. I couldn't stop either one.

By the end of the day on October 21st, I was contracting hard. I lay in the only place I couldn't stain: the bathtub. I spent the wee hours of the night on the hard, cold, uncaring porcelain. I was surprised that such a small baby could force my body into intense contractions that lasted for hours. When pain leads to grief instead of a tiny bundle of joy, birthing pains seem unbearable to endure. I was giving birth to death. There would be no smiles, no joy, and no celebration at the end of this agonizing purging work my body was doing.

I birthed our tiny baby there in the middle of empty screaming loud darkness. My husband sat on the cold tile head draped awkwardly on the edge of the tub. He rubbed my back with his tired, outstretched arms. There is nothing comfortable or kind about a lifeless baby being forced from its mother.

The pain and the bleeding got worse. We called our doctor and used the remaining five minutes left on our calling card. He told us to go to a hospital immediately. I was losing too much blood.

But it was the middle of the night. We had no idea where the hospital was in this unfamiliar place. We had no idea how long it would take to get there. There was no internet, no smart phones, no family or friends nearby. Our son was asleep. In a daze, we concluded that staying put was the best option.

I delivered my dead baby right there in the cabin. The bleeding and the pain was intense, but I didn't suffer further complications. We were all alone. Just us, our precious toddler, our dead baby, and a boat load of hot tears and messed up emotions.

I was weak and lethargic. In hindsight, maybe we should have gone to the hospital the next day—but for what? I didn't want to see people and I knew it would be an out-of-pocket expense. We didn't have much of anything in our pocket in the first place so that option seemed off the table. I already lost what was important. Nothing else seemed to matter. We were so young and inexperienced. Lord have mercy, we were *so* young.

We didn't explore, hike, or play that week. We grieved. We didn't find rest on that beautiful, scenic mountainside and we didn't find rest with God. We wrestled with God. We were in shock. We attempted to keep our little boy occupied for a week stuck inside with the few toys we packed in his suitcase. We zoned out, numb and weary in disbelief.

Why here? Why now? God, you had the power to hold this off for just one week until we returned home. Could you not have done *that* much?

I glanced through the pages of the guest journal on the table in the entry before we closed the door on a pain-filled seven-day stretch. Entry after entry described gratitude for the restful, refreshing time spent at that cabin. Things experienced, places explored, trails hiked, beauty enjoyed, and even ways God ministered to their souls. God granted them rest. God showed them His goodness. It seemed as if God loved them more than he loved us. I wrote our own entry in the guest journal:

> We lost our baby here. I don't ever want to come back. This place will always represent pain. But we do appreciate your generosity in allowing us to stay.

-Cory, Amy, Drew

That's all I had in me. I couldn't muster up enough energy to fake it. Our baby died in that cabin. We drove back on those same windy mountain roads, back to the Denver airport where it all began. Where my baby started dying. Where Mr. Bow Tie wouldn't cough up wheels. We made it back home to Wisconsin after our nightmare of a vacation. The one that we saved money for. The one that devastated us to the core.

In the weeks that followed, we kept breathing. We got out of bed. We ate. We showered. My husband went to work. I took care of our son. Somehow the pain didn't kill us like we first thought it would. Our little boy kept giggling, and eventually we did too. Life kept going. The clock kept ticking. The sun kept rising. The stars kept shining. The birds kept chirping.

> *He gives strength to the weary and increases the power*
> *of the weak. Even young men stumble and fall but*
> *those who hope in the Lord will renew their*
> *strength, they will soar on wings like eagles, they*
> *will run and not grow weary, they will walk and not*
> *be faint.*
>
> — ISAIAH 40:29-31

It would be a long time before we soared again. It would be a long time before we could even think about running again. But we were able to walk without fainting. Day by day, hour by hour, God gave us strength to put one foot in front of the other. He gave us strength to breathe as we put our hope in Him.

Sometimes taking one more step without fainting is the most we can manage. Sometimes just getting out of bed qualifies as a good day. There are seasons like that. Some are very long seasons. We want to rush past that leg of the journey but we can't. This was one of those just-do-not-faint-take-one-more-step-then-another kinds of seasons for us.

I remember the presence of God through it all, even though I continued to wrestle with Him. I didn't understand it all then nor could I articulate it while I was going through it but years later I knew what it was: grace. Grace enough. Grace was there.

> *My grace is sufficient for you, my power is made*
> *perfect in weakness.*
>
> — 2 CORINTHIANS 12:9

We were weak and His grace was powerfully sufficient in the pain. We received *grace in daily doses.* Perfectly portioned doses of grace—just enough for each new day. His mercies were new every new morning for us too. Mercy for today and then mercy for the next today and every today that came after that.

Before this experience at the ripe age of twenty-four, I didn't have the maturity nor the miles logged with God yet to grasp that pain can coexist with grace. That mercy can coexist with mourning. We can hold one in each of our hands and that's okay. Before this experience, I classified those things separately. I thought pain and grace and mercy and mourning could only be experienced separately. Yet, during this season here I was feeling deep disappointment with God while at the very same time finding comfort with Him too.

*Daily Doses of Grace and Every New Morning Mercies.* That's how I describe life after losing our precious baby in that log cabin. The place where we went to celebrate life but ended up mourning it.

I'm not saying we got answers. I'm not saying we found refreshment. I'm not saying we received a miracle. We didn't get any of those things. We were still confused, still alone, still hurt. And yet, we were held together by *Daily Doses of Grace* poured out in perfectly portioned measures, just what we needed each day for *that* day. We may not have sensed God strong all the time but He *was* there. His mercies were too. God intervened so that our pain didn't kill us. So that our grief didn't stop our beating hearts and take our breath away like we thought it would. God didn't stop the pain but he did carry us *through* the pain.

There is no neat and tidy ending to this story. In fact, the story unfolds further in the next chapter. In the meantime, I hope our story brings you comfort for those times when you have experienced deep loss and confusion. There are no easy answers in these seasons. But grace and mercy is a guarantee. So is breath in our lungs. So is walking without fainting.

In seasons of grief, that counts as a good day.

---

**Choosing Sweetness: Going Deeper with God**

> *Though He brings grief, He will show compassion, so*
> *great is His unfailing love. For He does not willingly*
> *bring affliction or grief to the children of men.*

— LAMENTATIONS 3:32-33

> *Blessed is the man who trusts in the Lord, whose*
> *confidence is in Him. He will be like a tree planted*
> *by the water that sends out its roots by the stream. It*
> *does not fear when heat comes; its leaves are always*
> *green. It has no worries in a year of drought and*
> *never fails to bear fruit.*

— JEREMIAH 17:7-8

*Though the mountains be shaken and the hills be removed yet my unfailing love for you will not be shaken nor my covenant of peace be removed says the Lord who has compassion on you.*

— ISAIAH 54:10

- What was your first big test of faith? Can you look back and see both the grace and the pain there together?
- In what ways was God's grace poured out day-by-day to you? If you're currently in that kind of pain, can you ask God to show you his perfectly portioned grace being poured out to you?
- Is there a season of your life where you struggle to understand God's timing? Why He didn't intervene or hold something off for just a bit?
- Make your own honest journal entry. It just may be the beginning of your own healing. Say it. Acknowledge what you lost and how it makes you feel. God can handle it.

———

SWEET NUGGETS: TAKEAWAYS TO REMEMBER

*Pain will not kill you. You will be held together by Daily Doses of Grace and Every New Morning Mercies.*

*In seasons of grief, walking without fainting is a good day.*

*Mercy can co-exist with mourning.*

*God carried me through the pain. He didn't stop it but He was in it.*

# 12

# PAIN BIRTHS BEAUTY

$\mathcal{M}$onths after losing our baby in that cabin, my friend Faye and I went swimming early one morning. We were at a usually vacant, slightly run down (okay, *very* run down) nearby motel. It was the kind of place where you're certain shady things are going down—but, hey, the pool passes were dirt cheap.

We were swimming laps. I use the term "laps" loosely—I mean a glorified doggy paddle. I'm not a swimmer, but I can doggy paddle like nobody's business and hang out floating on my back while the paint dries. (Make that a *second* coat of paint. Women have built-in buoys you know. Girl bonus.)

We could see the entire pool area at all times. No one else was usually ever there, except for this one morning.

We noticed a man sitting on the very end of a lounge chair with his feet on the edge of the pool. He looked like he was either praying or sleeping. We never saw him walk in. He sat there, very still.

Even though we were in a shady motel, neither I nor my friend felt afraid for some reason. We continued swimming. After several more minutes of swimming, Faye and I decided we were less interested in paddling and more interested in relaxing in the sauna, mainly so we could talk more easily, girlfriend-style. (It never was about the exercise, anyway. But our husbands didn't need to know that. *Shh.*)

We opened the sauna door, stepped inside, and sat down on the worn wooden bench. The man yanked open the door only moments later. He looked me in the eyes and said calmly, yet with great authority:

"You need to get out of here. You're pregnant."

The door slammed shut as he turned to leave. We bolted out of the sauna, but he was already gone. There was no possible way he could have traversed the distance from the sauna to the pool door in that short amount of time.

Faye and I both knew instantly: He was an Angel sent by God. He had to be. Nothing about the demeanor of this man made us think he was some kind of nutcase. He radiated pure calm and peace. Either he was some sort of divine being or a supernaturally fast, mysterious, prophetic man used by God. Either way the interaction was surreal, amazing, beautiful, and strange. I have never experienced anything like it before or since.

I drove home immediately with my wet bathing suit still on and hair sopping wet to take a pregnancy test. Sure enough, he was right.

I was pregnant.

I *had* encountered a divine messenger in that run down, sketchy motel where now I knew strange things most definitely *did* happen.

And guess what? Our due date was October 21st! On the exact same day of the year that God allowed our last child to die, a year later he would give us a new gift.

It was too precious, too personal, too perfect.

It was too much kindness for my tender little God's girl heart to even comprehend. I felt so loved. I felt so seen by God.

He cared about me, about us, and about our family, so much so that he sent a messenger to protect the baby in my womb from the dangerous heat of the sauna. He chose to heal our hearts in the most tender of ways. I was overcome with the goodness of God towards us.

Weeks later we went to a routine prenatal doctor's appointment. We made small talk while our doctor fiddled around with his stethoscope.

I saw it first on the doctor's face.

His brows furrowed. He got tense. He wasn't so chatty all of a sudden. I knew something was terribly wrong. He searched for our baby's heartbeat. *It was there. It had to be. He would find it. Right? Please, God, let him find it.*

I mean, an angel told me I was pregnant. Everything *has* to be okay.

The room became still and silent. We all knew exactly what was happening without anyone even saying a word. The doctor searched for our baby's heartbeat for almost an hour. His nurse came in a few times to tell him several other patients were waiting. She got the message not from his words, but from his countenance: This is all that matters right now. I swear the fire alarms could have blared and he wouldn't have stopped searching.

*Find it, please.* All three of us were silently praying, pleading, begging and believing for way longer than medically reasonable. But when three Christians are in a room, medically reasonable takes a back seat to what you believe is miraculously possible. We left room for God to do something. With exhaustion coupled with resignation in his voice our doctor said, "I'll order an internal ultrasound."

We slumped into chairs in the narrow busy hallway waiting for an exam room to open up. Our little boy played with a few toys the nursing staff had brought us to occupy him.

Forty-five minutes went by when I noticed a little etch-asketch toy. The kind with the magnetic pen that you write with and can erase with a swipe of a bar at the bottom. I picked it up. I sat with it in my lap for some time, staring at it. I finally mustered the courage to write what I knew I must:

"God, I give you my baby. Bye bye, sweet child. Mommy loves you."

Moments later the nurse approached saying the room and the machine were finally ready. Resigned to the will of God, and with a tad bit of newfound energy, I hopped up on the table hopeful that everything was actually going to be fine. They turned on the monitor.

There she was, our precious baby. That was the first time we had seen her and I fell so in love. Energy filled my veins. She was right there after all. We could see her! She wasn't gone or lost at all. She was right there, safe inside of me.

I reached my hand out towards the monitor. Tears of sweet gratitude and love burned down my cheeks. The technician turned the screen away from me. I realized only then that no one else in the room was happy except for me. My husband, the nurse, the doctor, and the technician all had a somber look on their faces. I saw my child but all anyone else in the room saw was what was missing: a beating heart. They knew what I couldn't process in that moment. The precious child in my womb I was looking at on the monitor was dead.

My husband ran his fingers through my hair as I lay there on the table trying so hard to get my spinning head around what was happening. Joy and love, shock and grief, were colliding in my heart like a deadly, bloody, horrible train wreck and I didn't think I could take another breath. My life was collapsing hard and fast. My body felt like it was hot and burning up from the inside out. I wanted to scream.

The doctor suggested they perform a D&C. That's a vacuum-like procedure where they rip the baby apart sucking and scraping the baby out of the mother's womb. He knew I lost a lot of blood the last time and this was the safest route. I couldn't make that decision right then. We asked for time. A day or two and more tests to be sure. He understood.

The staff left the room but we didn't. We were numb. What just happened? How do we gather up ourselves to leave? Where is the exit? What do we do next? We sat in the exam room, broken and immobile. Twenty minutes passed and the sweet nurse had to peek in to kindly ask us to vacate the room. They needed the room for other patients. *Oh yeah, other patients.* Other people. We felt like the only people on the planet in those moments. Actually, the planet had stopped rotating and time stood still. Not once did it cross our minds in those moments that they needed that room for anything else but our broken family.

We went home. I curled up in my husband's lap in the fetal position. He held me while we both sobbed.

In the weeks that followed, I began to think God had been cruel to us.

I didn't think God was supposed to be mean. But it sure seemed like he was being mean on purpose.

The due date? The pool guy? *Was* he an angel after all? What was the point of all this? *God, if you knew our baby would die why give us those precious details? Why even tell me at all?*

Hours after we got home, Faye, the same friend I went swimming with, came over to our house. She was that kind of kindred spirit. She just knew I needed her. With the absence of nearby family, she was a mother of sorts to me.

I was sitting in a rocking chair, rocking back and forth with my hand on my tummy, taking care of my baby. She was still in my womb. They told me she was dead but my mommy heart said she was still mine to care for. She was still part of me. My friend knelt by my side while she prayed and rubbed my feet.

The next day we went back to the clinic. Further tests confirmed what we already knew. I walked into the hospital a pregnant woman with my baby nestled in my womb and I walked out four hours later after having my dead child vacuumed out like she was an unwanted mass of nothingness.

She wasn't nothing. She was everything to me.

I thought God was acting more like a bully than a Father.

We went to church. (You have to when your husband is a pastor, whether you want to or not.) My husband, our little boy, and I sat down in a pew together. A young couple with a newborn came toward us and I sucked my still bloated stomach in to make room for them to pass by. The mom plopped down right next to me with her baby.

My head started to spin. I felt hot. My husband held me up during worship. My strength was sapped. I was broken before I got to church, and now God was kicking me while I was down. I felt like God didn't want my heart to heal. He wanted me a broken mess. He liked me being sad. He was even mean to me in church.

*God, I came to worship you in the midst of my pain. I showed up in spite of the fact that you allowed this hurt and all the seeming unnecessary details that were supposed to be happy that ended up so sad that came along with it. And this, this is how you show mercy? I crawled my way into church to worship you and you slap me in the face. Do you hate me? Do you like being mean to me? Do you love that woman more than me?*

In the midst of those early days of mourning, a few people offered their opinion on why I lost two children in a row:

"God must not like the name you picked out. That's why your babies are dying."

"You must have sin in your life. That's why your babies are dying."

"If you have ever spoken a single negative word about having another baby, then you killed your child because you know the Bible verse which says our words have the power of life and death. That's why your babies are dying."

Those words were like salt poured in an open, bloody wound. Despair beat at my door for a long time. My mantra of *Grace in Daily Doses and Mercies New Each Morning* was a lifeline I could barely grip on to in those days. We had been *here* before. We got through *that* alive. I knew that. But how can we do this again? Why is God allowing it again? Where is your mercy, God?

We survived those months like we had before. Pain didn't kill us this time, either. We eventually made it through. Not around, not over, but *through*. There was no stopping the pain or bypassing the pain. We had to go through the pain. I still have no easy answers, no formula, no cheap pieces of advice. We just made it through. We kept walking with God every day. Even when we were mad at Him. Even when He seemed cruel. Even though it felt like he teased us. He was committed to keep us from fainting while we were committed to keep on walking.

Months later we became pregnant again. We were cautiously optimistic yet completely terrified. I waffled between those two feelings every few minutes, I suppose.

Two months before our child was to be born, a man cornered me in our baby's nursery as I came out of our bathroom during our annual church Christmas open house. The man told me he had a message from God that he was to deliver to me:

"God wants me to tell you that your child will be severely handicapped but He will be with you through it."

I put my hand over my mouth and burst into silent tears because I knew I couldn't make a scene. My entire house was filled with guests. I felt my knees buckling. My same kindred spirit, lap swimming friend Faye happened by God's grace to be at our house at the time. I peeked around the corner into the living room. Cory was occupied with guests (plus he has no peripheral vision whatsoever) but my dear friend saw me (like women always do) and came right away.

Right there in the baby's nursery, the one with cute little sheep stenciled all the way around, walls painted a happy yellow, the one we had been anticipating bringing three babies home to by this point, right where the man delivered this horrifying message, she prayed over me. She rubbed my arms in a downward motion like she was casting off his message from me, my baby and my mind. She assured me that isn't how God would deliver a message if it was from Him. She told me not to receive it. She didn't buy it. It wasn't from God.

I borrowed her faith and took a deep breath. I pulled myself together. I fixed my raccoon eyes, blew my nose, stepped back into the party, and proceeded to put out more cheese and crackers. (Yes, after washing my hands. I got ya.) I wasn't going to let Satan have a field day with my heart. My sound mind was on the line. It was mine to keep and Satan could take a hike as far as I was concerned. I was tired of his company.

My husband and I chose not to do anything with this alleged prophecy. We processed the immediate fear the messenger imposed on us (oddly enough, he never returned to our church after that day) and then agreed he was absolutely right about one thing: God would be with us. Yes, He would.

We left the rest at the feet of the Father. Our Good, Good Father. Through all of the pain and questions we chose to declare He was good. He really was. His love was great too. So were his compassions. The prophet Jeremiah's words rang in my ears. Though all we had hoped for from the Lord was gone we could call to our minds truth, victory, hope, and peace. We weren't seeing God's compassions yet we declared Him compassionate. He didn't seem really loving but we declared that His love was great. I didn't know what to make of His faithfulness in those months but we thanked Him for being faithful, nevertheless.

We had no desire to know if what that strange messenger man said was true. It didn't matter. We wouldn't live in fear. *Not today Satan. I'm so sick of you.* Satan is good at what he does I will give him that. But creative, he is not. He uses the exact same methods since the days in the garden: lies and fear. Come on, man. Is that all you got?

Two months later, God blessed us with a healthy baby girl, Alexis Cori. (And even if she would not have been healthy, we still would have been blessed.) Her name means "helper of mankind," and that she is.

My heart couldn't contain the love and joy we felt toward our precious gift. To this day, nearly two decades later, I look at our two daughters—the two we had after the two we lost—and I cry sometimes. I cry at the thought that if we had had the other two we likely wouldn't have these two. I can't imagine our family without my girls.

Our family is beautiful and precious and perfect to me. I do think about our two children waiting in heaven for a hug and kiss from their mommy. That day will come when Heaven is my home. After all these years, I now smile at the thought of them. I don't cry tears of sadness, not as much anyway. I miss them but I mainly cry tears of gratitude for *God's Daily Doses* of Grace and for *Mercies New Every Single Morning*, for His unexplainable sovereignty, and for eventual healing. For keeping us from fainting, as weak as we were. For giving us the ability to walk, shuffle, jog, run, and finally soar again. For all five of our kids, those here on earth and those in heaven.

We have not gone back to that little log cabin in the mountains of Durango, Colorado.

But maybe it's time we did.

I'd like a chance to write another entry in that guest journal:

God is the healer of broken hearts. God saw us through with His daily doses of perfectly portioned, poured out grace. Pain births beauty. Eventually it does. Our family is living proof. We came all the way back here twenty years later to declare that.

- Cory, Amy, Drew, Alexis, Allie . . . and our two precious kids waiting for us in Heaven

———

## Choosing Sweetness: Going Deeper with God

*He helps us in all our troubles, so that we are able to
help others who have all kinds of troubles, using the
same help that we ourselves have received
from God.*

— II CORINTHIANS 1:4

*Though you have made me see troubles many and
bitter, you will restore my life again.*

— PSALMS 71:20

*God has made everything beautiful in its time.*

— ECCLESIASTES 3:11

*For He wounds, but He also binds up; He injures, but
His hands also heal.*

— JOB 5:18

- Has anything beautiful come through the deep pain you have walked through?
- Is there someone who needs to borrow your faith for a while? How could you come alongside of them?
- Has God ever seemed mean to you? Can you see now that mercy and mourning can hang out together?
- Do you believe that God can see you through what you are walking through?

———

## CHOOSING SWEETNESS: GOING DEEPER WITH GOD

*God commits to keep me from fainting, as I commit to keep walking.*

*I will make it through this with His Daily Doses of Grace and Every New Morning Mercies.*

*Healing comes as I trust His unexplainable sovereignty over my life.*

*God is with me. I can tell the devil to take a hike.*

*Pain eventually births beauty.*

# WHEN GOD'S WORD IS NOT ENOUGH

One phone call can catapult your whole life off-course.

I'm talking about the kind of crisis that stops your life dead in its tracks. One that sucks the air right out of the room you're standing in. One that threatens to drown you in the darkness of utter despair. One that violently throws everything else in your life into the backseat. The kind of crisis that makes you scream, "This can't be happening."

You hope it's a bad dream. But every morning when you wake up you realize all over again:

This is real.

A few years ago I found myself consumed with circumstances over someone I love. The nightmare wasn't unfolding in my life, but every moment of each day it impacted me.

Have you ever experienced a loved one's darkness in a way that suffocated you in its blackness too? I can't share the details because, quite frankly, it's not my story to tell. I will say that what happened was devastating. And there wasn't anything I could do to help.

All I could do was weep and pray.

*When Jesus saw her weeping, and the Jews who had*
*come along with her also weeping, He was deeply*
*moved in spirit and troubled. "Where have you laid*
*him?" He asked. "Come and see, Lord," they replied.*
*Jesus wept.*

— JOHN 11:33-35

Jesus wept over a dead man He was about to raise back to life. Why would Jesus cry over something He was about to fix? Scripture says Jesus loved Mary, Martha, and Lazarus. He cried because the people He loved were crying. He hurt because they hurt. Their tears gave way to His.

Sweet friends, God hurts with you when you're hurting. Please believe that. I sensed Jesus was weeping over my loved one's situation too. Maybe that sounds silly to you. If God cared enough He would do something, right? I do not believe Jesus is cold or unmoved by our pain. Our broken hearts touch His.

Perhaps someone you love has been in a serious accident. Or your adult child has been served divorce papers. A nasty custody battle over precious kids has ensued. Or your daughter's fiancée was killed. Or your child's diagnosis has changed her life and yours forever. Or a loved one is going to prison. Or your husband is cheating. Or your niece has disappeared. Or your grandchild was assaulted. Or your husband revealed to you he is gay.

You got *the* call. It's now happening to *your* family . . . now what?

We pray. We hope. We plead. We fight. We hold on. Right?

But for how long? Really, how long? I'm just asking. What do you do with your heart when it becomes *afraid* of the answer God might give? What do you do with your soul when it's tormented with unspeakable fears? How long can you suit up for the raging battle for your mind? How long can you cling to fading hope that something will change? That things *will* get better? They have to get better. Right? How long do you believe that? How long can you be burdened for someone you love so much before *you* go crazy? How long can you stand the deafening silence from God? How many times can we pour out the same desperate prayer?

And for crying out loud, how many times can you blow your nose from the constant flow of tears? Thank you, Jesus, for Puffs Plus Lotion tissues. Lifesaver, really. If only we had a solution for swollen eyelids, though. My poor eyes. So many days during that time I looked like I had been in a fight, only I didn't get punched in the face—I got punched in my soul. I was in a fight for my sanity.

What now? What do we do here? In this broken place with our weary soul, swollen eyes, and worn out voice, barely hanging on?

The patent Sunday school answer suggests, "Go to God's Word, cling to the Bible, find a promise and speak it like you mean it!"

And that's right. We should do those things. Yes. I'm in the habit of doing those things.

But today, for right now, for this crisis, for this, it isn't enough. I'm sorry. You will need to forgive me, but I'm going to say it: The Bible . . . it's just not enough this time. It's not.

In times of crisis, sometimes the Word hurts. Some verses sting. The words seem cruel and empty, when they are not working in my crisis. Maybe they come true for other people in similar situations but they are not coming true for our family. How do I know what is a promise in the Bible and what is a principle? When is the Word speaking of the here and now, when is it speaking of the then and there? It's all so confusing when a crisis is raging and your mind is reeling.

I often want to approach the Bible like it's a catalog. I want to flip through it, pick what I like, place a quick, hassle-free order. I want it delivered to my doorstep the very next day, thank you very much. I won't accept substitutions. I want the exact product that I ordered. And a promo code would be swell. Free shipping too.

I can quote Scripture about God healing the sick, rescuing the poor, releasing the captives, feeding the hungry, reviving the dead, punishing the wicked, or securing victory for the upright. But it doesn't mean He will. *Oh, He can!* And, at times, He does. But it doesn't mean He always will. Not *now* anyway, not on this side of Heaven.

Can I be honest about what I'm feeling right now in the middle of this raging crisis that isn't getting better?

God's Word is not enough. In times like this, I need God *Himself.*

I need Him. I need His presence. I need His power *in* me. I need His strength flowing *through* me. I need His hope *infused* in my very soul. I need to experience His peace that surpasses this thing. I need His peace *to* surpass this thing, or I will lose my stinkin' mind.

I need to experience His grace being sufficient while this nightmare rages on. I need to experience His mercies new each day while nothing new happens in my circumstances.

When His Word doesn't work, He does. I need Him.

I need to experience the actual Holy Spirit dwelling within my heart. I'm not interested in simply a promise on a page. What I need most is not a verse I claim over and over in some kind of Prosperity Gospel Hail Mary or a passage I demand God bring to my doorstep now or else I will be disappointed.

I need my God.

I need my Everlasting Father.

I need my Prince of Peace.

I need my Wonderful Counselor.

I need my Ever Present Help.

I need the Shelter of His Wing.

I need the Strong Tower
I need the Rock of Refuge
I *love* God's Word. I'm *in* God's Word. The Word *is* God. I know that stuff—I do. I speak God's Word out loud, often and with boldness. I tape paper with scriptures written on them all over my house—on my banister, on the mirrors, above the sink, and on my walls. I carry around spiral bound index cards plastered with Bible verses on them. God's Word is important and powerful.

But for me, especially in a crisis, being in God's Word isn't an exchange, and neither is it exactly the same, as being with the *Author of The Word Himself.* Am I making any sense? Does the difference resonate at all with you? If you're in or have been in a nightmare kind of crisis, then I believe you do.

This girl needs her Abba Daddy. I need a nap on His lap. I need to be tucked under the Shelter of His Wing for a bit. I need a bedtime story and a kiss on the forehead. I need Him to shut my lights off and tell me, "Sleep well tonight, sweetie." I need to lay my head on His chest. I need Him to rub my back and tell me that He loves me to the moon and back and everything is going to be okay.

At bedtime I repeat over and over in a hushed voice, "Jesus, Jesus, Jesus," just to calm my mind. To keep the torment from threatening to strangle me breathless as I lay in stillness and darkness on my bed. Nighttime is a vulnerable time for our minds. Once you fall asleep it's a relief. But it's the getting there that can do you in.

After months of living in this nightmare, I came to this conclusion: If God chooses to answer my request the way I want Him to, in the way his Word says He can, that will be an added blessing, but it's no longer what my heart clings to. Promises fulfilled are not what I'm desperate for anymore. God is. He is who and what I seek. He is who and what I need. He is the answer.

And Jesus reminded me of something I had forgotten in the early weeks of this nightmare. Something that would make or break me while I process someone else's pain: God won't give me grace for anyone else's life. Only mine. He won't give me grace to dwell on what it might be like to be in my loved one shoes. He gives me grace for living in my own shoes and He expects me to believe that He is doing the same for the one I love.

God won't reward us when we are somewhere we are not supposed to be. This includes our minds. When our minds are anxious and worried, ruminating on things it should not, and we flippantly ask for peace. Why do we then wonder why we don't have it?

> *He will keep in perfect peace him whose mind is*
> *steadfast (stayed on) thee.*

> — ISAIAH 26:3

God says He will give me His peace if my mind is steadfast. That's the deal. God won't keep me in perfect peace if my mind is running wild. If I'm dwelling on dread, worry, fear, and stress, why would I think God would reward me in that moment by giving me peace when I do nothing to maintain a sound mind?

God wants me to leave that place of negativity. If your child goes somewhere you have warned her not to go, you would want her miserable. Right? Why? So she would high tail it out of there. Peace is given to us when we high tail it out of worry. God told us not to go there. He told us to keep our minds steadfast and take our thoughts captive.

Two of my aunts lost their husbands when they were in their twenties. They had children ranging from infants to four years old. I obsessed about this when I was a young mom. If it happened to two of my aunts who is to say it won't happen to me? God didn't spare my aunts even though they both loved Him. Why would I presume God would spare me?

I pondered over and over how my aunts made it through those years. How did my cousins deal with the losses of their daddies? My grandparents watched two of their daughters walk through incredible agony. How on earth? I was sad over something God had already seen them through. Tormented over something that wasn't actually happening in my own life. I was thinking about what it was like living in someone else's shoes.

God whispered to me:

"Amy, yes, those were painful horrible days for your family. Your cousins missed their daddies very much. They still do. But here's the deal, I carried them through every day. I won't give you peace if you keep dwelling on this to the point of fear. I don't want you to stay in this thinking. Time to turn around and hike it out of here. Rely on me. Be with me. I assure you, I will give you grace for your life. Everyday. No matter what comes. But not until it comes. That's the deal. Keep that mind of yours fixed on me. Stayed on me. Steadfast and sound. Then I will give you peace. Don't go somewhere you're not supposed to be in that sweet but stubborn noggin of yours then wonder why you're miserable and tormented. I'd want you to know you need to leave. No peace without right-thinking. That's the deal."

God gives us grace for our own life. He then expects us to believe He is in the business of doing the same for the people we love. You won't be able to wrap your mind around the crisis someone else is enduring. You won't be able to grasp *how* they are making it through. You don't need to. All you need to know is that God's grace *is* meeting them in the middle of their own life just like He is meeting you in yours. Be there to support, to love, to pray with, to encourage, to help but don't take on the pain God isn't giving you the grace to live through.

I began to believe that God was with my loved one. That He would be sufficient for every moment. I had to stop thinking about what they were going through and start thanking God for seeing them through. I had to accept that God wasn't going to give me grace for someone else's life.

Did you know that you have permission to have a good day even if someone you love is not? That just might be the one thing God wanted someone to hear through this book. If that's you, feel free to toss this in the Goodwill pile now. Seriously, it is that important that some of us grasp this. When one of your people is struggling miserably you don't need to be miserable too. We need to mourn with those who mourn, yes! Please continue to be empathetic and caring. But if you're one of those people with an extra tender heart, make sure you don't take on pain you're not actually going through. And if you have a good day when the one you love is not, consider it a precious gift from God. Be grateful without feeling guilty.

There was a familiar passage that spoke volumes to my soul in those crisis days:

> *God is our refuge and strength an ever present help in*
> *time of trouble. Therefore we will not fear though*
> *the earth give way and the mountains fall into the*
> *heart of the sea, though its waters roar and foam*
> *and the mountains quake with their surging . . . Be*
> *still and know that He is God.*
>
> — PSALM 46

These verses have taken on fresh meaning to my soul since the crisis enveloped us. Prior to the nightmare that has kept us on our knees battling the enemy for peace while also resolving to maintain some semblance of normality in our home, I focused solely on God being our help in time of trouble. I like those words. They feel good.

I want to know that God will help me in my trouble.

Problem was, I included a few words not mentioned: *He will get me out of trouble. He will fix my trouble. He will stop the trouble.* But unfortunately none of those phrases are found. The verse says, He is our help in times of trouble.

Actually, if we keep reading Psalm 46, we find some serious trouble.

The earth gives way.

The mountains fall into the sea.

The waters roar and foam.

The mountains quake.

It doesn't get much worse than the earth giving way beneath us. Ever felt like it has? Or like it's about to? Yeah. Me too.

So what about all those verses that pronounce God being our help, strength and refuge? What help is God when you find yourself beneath the rubble of an earthquake, or riding the surging waves of a storm, or clinging to a rock that's sliding into the sea?

I read the verses again. Two words from Psalms 46 grab my soul this time:

Ever present.

That's it. Right there. That is what I overlooked countless times before.

He is my Ever Present. That's the help! His guaranteed presence in the disaster. He is my refuge and strength, an ever present help in trouble.

The Presence of the Almighty God of the Universe is with me. His presence is unshakable and unmoving. He is available and everlasting. He is with me. Near me. On me. In me. God doesn't bring us some kind of refuge. He *is* the refuge.

With His presence we need not fear or panic in the midst of trouble. He is with us in it.

So, let the earth give way, let the mountains fall into the sea, let the waters foam, roar and surge around me. I need not fear. I can Be Still and Know that He is indeed God and that God Almighty is Ever Present with me through it.

He is my help.

When God's Word doesn't deliver on what seems like promises on its pages, I tell you what, God *does*. He delivers every single time. On time. To your front door, immediately. No waiting. No substitutions. He is ever present. That means always. That means He isn't going anywhere. That means He never plays hooky or calls in sick. He never sleeps in; in fact, He never sleeps. So you can, sweet one. Go ahead and get some rest. God is awake and in control. He's got this. He's got you. He's got the one you love. That's comforting to this girl in the midst of a crisis over someone I love so much.

Yeah, the earth is giving way beneath my feet but God is here with me. I don't need to fear. Neither do you.

## CHOOSING SWEETNESS: GOING DEEPER WITH GOD

*When I am afraid I will trust in you.*

— PSALM 56:3

*Have mercy on me O God, for in you my soul takes refuge.*

— PSALM 57:1

*So do not fear, for I am with you; do not be dismayed, for I am your God. I will strengthen you and help you; I will uphold you with my righteous right hand.*

— ISAIAH 41:10

151

- Does it feel like God has hurt your feelings by not coming through for you like it seems His Word promises He will?
- Have you been waiting for a long time to see improvements in a crisis you're experiencing? Talk to God about that.
- Do you see the difference in seeking the presence of the Author of the Word and seeking the Word? How can you do both?

———

## CHOOSING SWEETNESS: GOING DEEPER WITH GOD

*God hurts when I hurt. He is not unmoved by my pain.*

*God will not reward me when I'm somewhere I should not be.*

*God's grace is meeting the ones I love in the middle of their life just like He is meeting me in mine.*

*I will not take on pain that God is not giving me the grace to live through.*

*God is awake and in control. I can go ahead and get some rest.*

*When His Word doesn't work like I want it to, He does.*

## SHOW UP FOR MY LIFE

*a*s five girlfriends who had not had time for a good talk in months, we found ourselves with the rare chance to be together and get real.

We went to the only quiet room in the house, the one where the kids wouldn't find us. Piled on the bed, we were like college students in a dorm, but well aware that life was far too real and raw now to still be like those carefree days.

We poured open our hearts. After forty years of living, there's a whole lot to cry over and a whole lot to laugh about. We shared unreservedly. We cried because we couldn't help it. We prayed because that's the only thing we knew to do.

"This isn't what I had planned . . . . This isn't what I had dreamed life would be . . . . This isn't what I wanted . . . . I don't like this assignment . . . . This is too much . . . . It's not right . . . . It's not fair . . . . This hurts . . . . I wish things were different . . . ."

Unwed pregnancies, pornography addictions, betrayal, jobs lost, kids struggling with disabilities, chronic diseases, raising kids through the grueling teen years, financial hardships, hurting relationships, childhood baggage, issues with parents and churches and people and car mechanics and leaking roofs and flooded basements, deaths of loved ones, pain over words, pain of broken bodies, dashed dreams . . . .

It never ends, does it?

Sitting there together talking, we were having ourselves what I call a "Hagar Moment." Hagar was a slave. She didn't picture her life turning out how it was either.

> *Now Sarai, Abram's wife, had borne him no children.*
> *But she had an Egyptian maidservant named*
> *Hagar; so she said to Abram, "The Lord has kept me*
> *from having children. Go, sleep with my*
> *maidservant; perhaps I can build a family through*
> *her." Abram agreed to what Sarai said. So after*
> *Abram had been living in Canaan ten years, Sarai*
> *his wife took her Egyptian maidservant Hagar and*
> *gave her to her husband to be his wife. He slept with*
> *Hagar, and she conceived. When she knew she was*
> *pregnant, she began to despise her mistress. Then*
> *Sarai said to Abram, "You are responsible for the*
> *wrong I am suffering. I put my servant in your*
> *arms and now that she knows she is pregnant she*
> *despises me. May the Lord judge between you and*
> *me." "Your servant is in your hand," Abram said, "Do*
> *with her whatever you think is best." Then Sarai*
> *mistreated Hagar; so she fled from her. The angel of*
> *the Lord found Hagar near a spring in the desert; it*
> *was the spring that is beside the road to Shur. And*
> *he said, "Hagar servant of Sarai, where have you*
> *come from, and where are you going?" "I'm running*
> *away from my mistress Sarai," she answered.*
>
> *— GENESIS 16:1-8*

Even though this whole mess was Sarah's idea in the first

place, I have a hunch that Sarah didn't truly *want* her husband doing what she told him to do.

I'm going to guess that Sarah was likely emotional over the ongoing pain of facing infertility. It could have also been *that* time of the month, when hormones and emotions wreak havoc on most females. Do you think it's possible that what she was really after when she made that suggestion to her husband was reassurance? Maybe all she needed him to say was:

"No way, baby, I'm a one-woman man! I love you. I want you no matter what. I trust God. I'm the Father of Faith after all. I know He will fulfill His promise to us. We're in this together. It's going to be okay. No, I won't sleep with any other woman! Don't be ridiculous! Eat some chocolate if you need to, buy a new sweater or a new throw pillow, get yourself a *fu-fu* coffee if that's what it'll take but please, honey, pull yourself together! Don't utter such nonsense."

Abraham goes along with his wife's plan only to be blamed for it later. He's not the only husband that has had to deal with an irrational wife (I'm living proof of that statement). Sarah held her man responsible for the disaster created as a consequence of something she asked for (ah, still raising my hand). Sarah resented the very thing she *had to have* in her season of despair.

You know, before she makes a decision, a wise woman asks herself if she will be glad tomorrow that she had *this* today. How many of us wake up the morning after a purchase, a date, a buffet, a slot machine, a bag of chips, a conversation and think, "Boy, I sure wish I had not insisted on having that yesterday." A *beautiful* woman, who is *grown up* in Christ, seeks wise counsel and is careful about making decisions while she is in a season of despair (or in a week of raging hormones).

After Abraham got Hagar pregnant, the house got *ugly*. Of course it did. Sarah makes Hagar's life more miserable than it already was. Sarah was downright cruel to her. So Hagar runs away. I would have too. Hagar was distraught. Her life wasn't right. Things weren't fair. She had been wronged. She was ripped from her family and her own people in Egypt, sold as a slave, and now violated. Life was painful. This isn't what she dreamed her life would be like.

God does what God always does for His kids. He shows up to her in the desert and says to her, "Hagar, servant of Sarah, where have you come from and where are you going?"

God just goes there, doesn't He? He calls her the very name that makes her cringe, the one she deeply resents: "Servant of Sarah." Oh, you can bet that stung. God wasn't taunting her, but He wasn't afraid to dive right in and make Hagar process her reality and the pain that went along with it.

Listen, you can be assured that God will only bring up what He is willing to bind up, no matter how uncomfortable that makes us in the moment. After all, we can't make progress over something we refuse to process.

He asks her where she's come from and where she is headed. He already knew the answer, of course. But sometimes God wants us to hear ourselves say it. You know, say what's *really* wrong. Hagar tells the angel that she is running away from Sarah.

God responds back to her with—are you ready for this? Seriously, like this is a good time to take a chug of Diet Coke if that's your thing. It's mine. (Although La Croix is actually growing on me. I know! Can you believe it?)

*Go back to Sarah and submit to her.*

— GENESIS 16:9

Say what, now? You really didn't mean that, did you, God? (There has got to be a typo in my Bible. Please tell me yours says something different.)

I mean, God, what you *meant* to say was:

"Oh sweet honey, my poor precious baby girl. I'm so sorry. I can't believe what these meanies are doing to you. I'm going to pluck you up out of that terrible life and plop you down in a place you deserve. A place where you will be loved, wanted, and treated properly. I will fix everything for you. No more Sarah. No more Abraham. No more slavery. No more meanies ever! I won't tolerate anything in your life being unfair or wrong. With a snap of my finger, I will change everything and make it all better!" *Insert kiss on her forehead and a glass of milk with two Oreos.*

No, I'm afraid that isn't at all what God said to her.

Instead He told her to go back. Face it. Accept it. Live it well.

(But, dear one, if you're in an abusive relationship, then you need to get out and get help. God is not suggesting you stay in a dangerous place.)

If we read between the lines I think God is *actually* saying:

"My precious, sweet girl, here's the deal. You live in a broken, messed up world. Things aren't right. Yucky, hurtful things are happening. Things I don't like. Things I don't approve of. Everyone experiences the consequences of other people's poor choices and sin. I can't change everything. Well, I can, but if I did, mankind would not have a free will. If I did, this would be heaven, but it's not. That is coming. But until then, life unfolds as people live it. No, this wasn't my plan A for your life. I didn't create you to be a slave. This wasn't my very best for you. Abraham and Sarah's decisions to own you and abuse you and your father's decision to allow you to be sold as a slave, changed that. But I'm with you. I'm here. I always will be. I see you. I came here so you would know that. I love you. I will right every wrong one day. I will use this for good in your life. I can redeem your days and bring blessing out of heartache. Go back. Live your life as a pleasing aroma to me. Honor me where you find yourself, fair or not. Honor me where you are whether it's what you dreamed it would be or not. Go back. Love me well. I will be with you and I will have eyes on you always. Now go, sweetie. You've got this."

God's words to Hagar are His same words to us: "My daughter, where are you going? What are you running from? Let's talk this through."

Okay, so you might not have physically run away like Hagar did, though some of us have. Others of us have shut down, pulled back, grown discontent, withdrawn, given up, resented, and resigned. We've thrown ourselves a big pity party, one with lots of chocolate, mind you. Maybe we emotionally ran away from a responsibility or a relationship. We pushed back from a calling or a position God has given us.

God invites us to just *say it*. Say what is on your heart and troubling your soul—all of it. Tell Him, already. For crying out loud, be real. Be honest. He can handle your deepest thoughts.

The reality was, there would be no greener grass for Hagar. Where did she think she would go? She was pregnant. She was a slave. Who would welcome her and take her in? And how would that be any different from her current situation? *Hagar, honey, where are you going?* Running won't bring the relief we are after, will it? The reality is if we want to get free of what is causing us pain, we will have to face it. God didn't say He liked it. He didn't say Hagar had to like it. But he did say go back and face it.

For some of us it's motherhood or the wife life we run from. We check out, give up, disengage. We pour ourselves into every other thing to distract and numb ourselves from the chaos, stress, and mundane life of home. It isn't what we dreamed it would be. It's so much harder. The dishes, laundry and toilet scrubbing are no fun. We stop giving our very best in our own homes.

If you're running, God's loving, fatherly voice is beckoning you to take off your cute running shoes. (Because they must be cute. If I'm going to work out I need to feel cute doing it. Anyone?) Our role is irreplaceable in our home. Let's show up for it. The years with our kids in our home fly by so fast. I'm twenty-two years in and only have a couple more left. A new stage of motherhood with adult kids begins soon. Motherhood is the very best thing that ever happened to me. Being a mom is hands down the greatest joy and the highest privilege of my life. It's my best work. It's my favorite work. It's my favorite thing to do, in fact. If you're a mom can I encourage you to be awake for all of it? You will be so very glad you were. I pinky promise. I plan to write a book on motherhood next. It's *that* important to me and moms are *that* precious to my heart.

Maybe we are running from seasons of singleness, infertility, the ongoing demands of having a special needs child or aging parents. It's easier to shut down than engage when there seems to be more withdrawals than deposits in our life. Running from it can feel like our only option when we have nothing left in our tank to keep going.

I know for me, it can be subtle some days. I can shut down and run away emotionally when I'm spent, stressed out, or hurting over a relationship. I can get lazy in my house and tired of the ongoing mess and meals to prepare. I can give up taking care of my body and my soul because there are so many other things clamoring for my attention. I can pull back from church when I find more exhaustion than refreshment there. Some days I want to crawl into a hole and stay hidden there.

Some days I really wouldn't mind at all if the world just stopped spinning long enough for me to get off the ride. No, I'm not suicidal. Sometimes I just feel like being done is all. If it were as easy as not inserting another quarter, I think I'd say, "Thank you, for the thrill ride, I'm good now." I love my life. I love my family. I live grateful each day for breath in my lungs and a body that works. It's not that I'm miserable. It's not that I'm depressed. (Well, some days I am.) It's just that sometimes I'm tired and ready to call it a day. I don't want to show up. I don't want to face everything any longer.

God never fails to meet me in the desert of my running with the same questions He asked Hagar all those years ago:

"So, where ya headed, Amy? What are you running from? And where exactly do you think you're going? You don't really think it'll be better else where do you? You do take yourself with you wherever you go, remember? The same issues and people you have in your life right now, you'll find them in a new place too. You do know that, right? The same people pop up everywhere because you expect them to be there. You have them all pegged before you even get to know them. Let's talk. Let's process what is on your heart. Running away never works. Same issue, new view: that's the only thing you will find. Live your life well right now, right here! In the midst of everything hard, show up. Wake up. Re-engage. And for crying out loud, stop drinking so much Diet Coke and shopping for bargains you don't need!"

But Diet Coke and bargain shopping . . . it could be worse, right? That's what I tell my husband, anyway.

Deep down I know there's nothing healthy about searching for distraction instead of engaging with my life. If I'm numb and checked out I will have no energy to deal with my stuff, seek healing, and gain a proper perspective. Those are the places where I'm *growing old* instead of *growing up*. *Bitter or sweet*—I have a choice. Live my life or run from it.

Friend, can we muster up the courage to go back to the places we have run from and honor God right here, right now? Can we decide to be the best version of ourselves where we are? To be alive and engaged with our life just *as it is*? There is no escaping our lives. That's called a "vacay." We get to do that about twice a year. For the rest of the fifty weeks, we gotta start showing up again.

You might not be where you wanted to be. I know. I get that. I can tell you that preacher's wife living isn't at all what I thought it would be, either. Being a mom isn't the walk in the park I expected it would be. Neither is the wife life in many ways, though I do love my man. I'm crazy about him, really. (And he does drive me crazy too. Funny how that works). Still, marriage isn't completely what I envisioned. But it's precisely where I am. So I best show up for it.

After God told Hagar to go back and submit to Sarah, He adds something. Listen to this:

> *I will also increase your descendants that they will be*
> *too numerous to count.*

— GENESIS 16:10

The angel goes on to speak words of prophecy over her son, which to Hagar was very good news. Her son would be a free man. He would not be bound as a slave. He would rule, lead, fight and have rights unlike she did. It's an interesting account but suffice it to say, this word of prophecy meant the world to Hagar as a hurting mom and a woman who was enslaved.

Seventeen years later Hagar and her son would be kicked out of their home (Genesis 21). Sent away with nothing more than a lunch box and water bottle, they end up, against all odds, surviving and starting a brand new life. (We'll talk about his story in my next book on motherhood.)

So when God encounters Hagar in the desert that day, He knew something she didn't know, this season of submitting to Sarah wouldn't last forever. God knew there was more to Hagar's life and future than *her*. There were greater purposes and plans ahead. In fact, Hagar had more going on in her life than being a mistress and she was far more than a slave. Sarah's power was on a leash even though she didn't know it.

Friend, maybe you have run from a bully like Sarah. Maybe it's a role or a title or a responsibility that's super hard. I'm here to remind you that there's more going on in your life than *that role* or *that person*. There is more to who you are too. Read that again if you need to. This season you're in? You won't be *here* forever. You will leave *this* at some point.

Promise me that you won't get mentally stuck in this difficult place. Maybe it's time we stop giving so much power to the Sarahs in our life. (If your name is actually Sarah, I do apologize. Just work with me here. You're loved I promise and no one thinks of you as a bully, okay? Good.) Maybe it's time we realize that our bullies don't get the final say over our lives, either. If they didn't design you they don't get to define you—period. They might think they can but, honey, be assured that their leash is short and your God has plans for you that they cannot thwart.

One more thought that I want to leave you with as we wrap up this chapter.

I was FaceTiming with my college-aged daughter and her besties when they began sharing with me that they felt guilty for their periodic struggle with discontentment. These girls love Jesus, a lot. They are mature in Christ. They love His Word. They are making wise decisions and following God's leading in their lives, yet they wrestle from time to time with where they are. As adult women, we can relate, can't we?

I have begun to wonder if we've confused our feelings of discontentment. Maybe we are mislabeling and therefore mistreating the symptoms. We feel shame for the unsettledness we feel. We vow to try harder to be a more content Christian. We hide our struggle from people out of embarrassment. After all shouldn't we be more mature, more grateful, more satisfied in Christ alone?

We continue to think we will find relief by filling our homes and our stomachs with more stuff. We continue to waste precious hours scrolling on our devices instead of being present in our lives. We beat ourselves up for feeling restless and unsatisfied. What if what we think is discontentment is really a longing for home? What if this feeling is actually a good thing?

Ecclesiastes 3:11 says God has set eternity in the hearts of all men. That means there's a longing for eternity, for heaven, in our hearts that God himself put there. Like a locket hung around our neck. It's a reminder. So we will never forget the greatest love of our life and the home He is busy building for us. God wants to be on our minds you know. He likes that very much. It's everything to Him.

Hebrews 12 tells us that we are aliens and strangers in a foreign land on a temporary assignment. Read that sentence again. Do you live like that? Are you aware that as children of the Maker and Master of this amazing Universe you're an alien here on earth? It feels funny to even type those words. But it's true. We live in a foreign land. Eternity is set in our hearts.

Our entire lifetime chugging air on this tiny planet is like a mist that vanishes, James 4:14 says. The Psalmist says we are a mere breath, our days are fleeting, our days vanish like smoke. God remembers that we are a passing breeze and the span of our years is as nothing before God. Philippians says our citizenship is in heaven. Corinthians says we groan, longing to be clothed with our heavenly dwelling.

We won't ever feel fully at home here. So you can stop expecting to. We are on a road trip of sorts, passing through this place. We were made for a different country. A country whose architect and builder is God. He's coming for us you know. To take us to the place where when we awake and see Him face to face, we will finally be satisfied (Psalm 17:15). The place where we will gaze upon His beauty as David said was the one thing he asked the Lord for and the one thing that he seeks (Psalm 27:4).

The more we get to know Him, the more we worship Him, the more we love Him, the more we will desire to be in His presence. Our desire, the one that God put in our hearts for eternity, it will grow more intense—not less. You will grow more unsettled with life on this foreign planet apart from Him. The more mature you are in Christ the less content you will be with the mere things this world offers. And that's a good thing.

That longing, that twinge that something is just not quite right, that ache you sometimes have that you label as a spirit of discontentment? Don't be bothered by that. You're likely homesick, is all. You're homesick for your Abba Father. You have fallen hard for Him, you know. Maybe it's an indicator that you have grown to know Him well. That you love Him like crazy. That your heart is actually very mature. So no need to feel amiss. No need to panic or feel guilty. No need to pack your duffle bag to run away from your imperfect life. It just comes with the territory of living on foreign soil.

Eternity awaits us. Where everything will always be perfect, painless, and more glorious and satisfying than we could even imagine. In the meantime, I'm pretty sure I can endure anything for this little trip I'm on because I get to go home real soon. So will you. Until then, when I get that discontented, something-is-just-off-but-I-don't-know-fully-why kind of feeling, I won't beat myself up. I will tell my little soul, "You miss your Daddy." I'll nestle back into my life, get back to living awake here and now in whatever season or reality I find myself in. Because that *then and there* is surely coming.

Hagar had courage to get back to her life. We can too. We've got this, girls!

Just a little while longer . . . .

---

## CHOOSING SWEETNESS: GOING DEEPER WITH GOD

*Yet, I am always with you. You hold me by my right hand. You guide me with your counsel and afterward you will take me into glory. Whom have I in heaven but you, and earth has nothing I desire but you. My flesh and my heart may fail, but God is the strength of my heart and my portion forever . . . it is good for me to be near God. I have made the Sovereign Lord my refuge.*

— PSALMS 73:23-28

- Are there any roles or responsibilities in your life that you have run from? In what ways have you run?
- Do you have a title that causes you pain or feelings of resentment? (Wife of a porn addict, mother of a wayward child, divorcee, stay-at-home mom, working mom . . . .)
- What would honoring God in the midst of your reality look like?
- When you feel discontent how do you attempt to ease those feelings?
- How do you process heaven being your true home and how does that impact how you feel while here on earth?

———

SWEET NUGGETS: TAKEAWAYS TO REMEMBER

*My role is irreplaceable in my home. I will show up for it.*

*Running away never works. I will have the same issues but with a new view. I will muster up the courage to go back to the places I have run from and honor God there.*

*Live my life well right here, right now.*

*Maybe my discontentment is really a longing for home. I miss my Daddy is all.*

*I can endure anything for this little trip I'm on because I get to go home soon.*

15

# THE LORD HAS BEEN GOOD TO ME

*W*e buried my husband's grandma one muggy June morning.

A couple of decades prior, Cory's grandparents sold their beloved family farm. Age had stolen their resolve to stay and a move into town was inevitable. With no family having the desire to take over the plow, there was no choice but to let it go.

As relatives gathered from across the country for the funeral, we knew this would likely be the last chance we'd have to spend time together at that old family farm. Even though someone else had owned it for years now, the owners didn't mind us visiting. We all made the trek down the dusty country road one last time.

We walked the barren land that once produced abundant crops, birthed brilliant flower beds, and cushioned little feet at play. We curiously opened the creaking door of the outhouse that was still standing after all these years. We cautiously stepped into dilapidated barns that once held cows and plows. We ran our hands along the weathered wooden fence. Everything was empty and still.

We laid eyes on that old white farmhouse that used to be home. It was now falling apart, unkempt, and lonely. The farm that once was bounding alive with family, kids, crops, gardens, chores, dairy cows, litters of kittens, and clothes pinned up drying in the wind, was now completely lifeless. The trail to the lake was gone. Trees and weeds had grown up, but so had we. Or, at least, I think we had.

While family members were bursting with memories of days of old, I was quiet. Pondering, soaking it all in, and hunting for treasures, for lost, unwanted things. Tin pails half buried in earth next to the water pump. An old metal mail box next to the barn, tangled in weeds. A white chipped up screen window lying in dirt in a dark corner of the tired barn. I could have hauled a trailer home with all the tossed aside, forgotten things I found.

Too timid to ask myself, my husband asked the owners if we could take these few pieces of "junk" home. "Take it, please," they said. They had no kids and no farmer instincts in their bones. Seems they just wanted space. So they bought the farm and let it die.

None of this junk needed rescuing. But I did. This stuff was symbolic to me. Unwanted, tossed aside, long forgotten, beat up things picked back up, dusted off, given new value.

I have felt those *tossed aside* pangs.

Something tells me you have too.

One time, a woman said to me in the crowded church foyer after church: "You're a terrible pastor's wife and awful women's ministry director."

For starters, I refused to adopt the woman's cat. (We had a cat once, and I guess he was pooping in our neighbor's mulch and our neighbor didn't appreciate that—at all. We did *not* need another cat.) Also, this woman was mad that I didn't agree to host foreign exchange students in our home for a year either. (I could hardly understand what my own teenagers were saying and they spoke English.) I also wouldn't agree to travel across the country to attend conferences with her three times a year.

So that Sunday she let me have it.

Another woman once told me: "You kicked Jesus out of our church." She had hung an odd looking painting of Jesus in the prayer room—it was quite scary looking. She wanted one put in each classroom too.

I wasn't the one who told her to remove the picture, but I was on the interior design team and I was the pastor's wife, so she blamed me. She also accused me of taking away her hymns along with her pews. (Oddly enough, I wasn't even the pastor's wife when the hymns and pews got the boot. Not even sure I was out of high school for that matter.) She said she had to apologize to Jesus on my behalf because I didn't want Him in the building.

She was certain she would die over the pain of it and insisted that if she had, that I'd have been responsible for her death.

Another time at a potluck, after I didn't sit down at her table, a woman said, "Do you think you're too good for us?"

I sat down at the first open table so I could feed my three hungry kids. That's it. Believe me, thinking I'm "too good" isn't my struggle. I have lots of struggles but that is certainly not one of them. I'm just trying to be a mom. We're just trying to eat lunch. (No, I didn't say any of that. I learned it's no use.)

One time, a man was incredibly degrading to me at the hardware store. He was mad at my husband for ten straight years and he took it out on me. I could never figure out why.

People criticized us for the way we educated our kids and made lots of drama over it. People left our church over our family's education choices.

A staff member at the middle school was harsh with our son because, like she told him, "I know who your father is." She was upset that we would put a café in our church. That was sacrilegious, I guess. So she left the church. Our son got the brunt of that one while trying to navigate middle school.

A church member was disappointed that I didn't commit to spending Sunday afternoons visiting the local women's prison. She concluded that meant I didn't have a heart for the prisoners like Jesus says we should. (Any afternoon, but Sunday, please.)

A woman complained to other people that the pastor's wife did not value missions because she wouldn't commit to attending a weekly ladies sewing club. (I do care about missions, but I'm bad at sewing. Can't those two things coexist?)

People told us it was wrong of us to have friends. No one should have an "in" with the pastor. We are normal people who need friendships but that isn't how some people see it.

A handful of men in leadership believed that I was sinful, unbiblical, and a poor example to young women because of my spiritual gifts, which resulted in nearly a decade of debates and regulations against women in ministry. A male pastor in our denomination said that I, along with women like me with the gifts of teaching and prophecy, are female devils. He told me we were causing the Jezebelic destruction of the church. (That seems a tad extreme, if you ask me.)

I was reprimanded for inquiring if my daughter was safe when she got injured on a mission trip. I was told that as the lead pastor's wife I should know better than to imply that our church doesn't trust the mission's organization or its leaders. I don't even have permission to be a mom—that hurt most of all.

I could go on, but I won't.

I'm sorry if that list was too much for you.

I think we are both tired. You have your own stories, don't you? I wish I could listen to your heart. I really do. Because your hurt matters. Your perspective matters. Your life matters.

As we walked around the old farm together, I felt like buying a farm and letting it die too—because that's how I felt inside. At that point in my life, I had grown scared of the church. I tried to put on a brave face, but on the inside I very much felt like the tossed aside, unworthy pieces of junk that I rescued at the farm that day. I thought I'd rust out and disintegrate right there. I didn't feel worthy of a rescue.

Some of you have been there too—verbally assaulted by someone who should have loved you, appreciated you, cheered for you. Maybe your husband, your boss, your pastor, your parents, your coach—someone you never thought would toss you aside, did. They were supposed to be on your team but they betrayed you. Boy, is that hard.

Or maybe you feel like the punching bag at your office or in your family. The one who takes all the hits and is forced to "fall in line" or else. Maybe you have been abused by a family member, which is horrifying enough, but now you also have the pressure of keeping the family peace. You may feel like your voice doesn't matter. Like your healing doesn't matter. And instead, protecting the perpetrator is all that matters—all in the name of the family's reputation.

Dear one, if that is you, my heart aches for you. Please know your life and your experiences do matter—very much so.

> *If an enemy insults me, I could endure it; if a foe were*
> *raising himself against me, I could hide from him.*
> *But it is you, a man like myself. My companion, my*
> *close friend with whom I once enjoyed sweet*
> *fellowship . . . .*
>
> — KING DAVID, PSALM 55:12-14

When one of your own people crushes your heart, it wounds you fiercely. Friendly fire is the most painful. David would concur.

These are the type of wounds that make us want to buy a farm. And let it die.

Other times it isn't an assault that makes us feel tossed aside. Sometimes things just change. Changes that come whether we like it or not and make us feel like that old buried pail lost under grass and weeds. Like old news or a has-been struggling with purpose and fulfillment. We wrestle with letting some good things go. Seasons when we felt like our talents were being utilized. That job we loved. The days when our kids needed us but now they don't even have time to call. Our marriage once thrived but now feels passionless. The church that felt like our family but stuff happened and now it isn't the same. Letting go of things that brought us a sense of identity and fulfillment is difficult. Sometimes when those seasons are over, so are we.

But the actual truth is, we are never truly tossed aside. *Oh, it may seem like it.* But let me tell you something, there's no person on this planet who has authority to cast aside what God created. No one has that much power. Even if they wish they did. Even if they think they do.

If someone didn't design you they don't get to define you. I just typed that for myself. Maybe you needed to hear it too.

Can I tell you one of the biggest game changers in my life? Seriously, like hands down the most effective rhythm change I implemented in my life that helped me get off the dying farm? The thing that has enabled me to consistently choose the road to *sweetness* rather than *bitterness?*

It starts with a verse. My daughter painted it on a piece of wood that now sits in my dining room. I look at it every day:

> *Be at rest once more, Oh my soul, for the Lord has been good to you.*

> — PSALM 116:7

Yes! He has!

I started a gratitude journal during this tossed aside time in my life. I was inspired by Ann Voskamp's book, *One Thousand Gifts*. Eight years have passed since I started recording all the ways God has been good to me. I hit #17,000 a few months ago. That's a lot of goodness isn't it?

I bet you could count your blessings that high too. When people are not good to us, God has been good to us. We can tell our souls to rest even when life has been hard. This is how I resist wallowing next to the dilapidated barn on a dying farm. This is how I convince myself to stay at it, to not give up, to keep living fully, freely and *beautifully*. This is how I keep my joy and my hope. Here are a few things on my list:

#1 walks in the freshly fallen snow

#25 daughters curled up cozy with books

#38 a warm cup of tea

#52 morning hugs

#101 lemon drops

#366 brownie batter on the chin of my eleven year old

#509 peeks of sunshine on a cloudy day

#1102 an evening walk with my man

#2046 birds chirping

#3769 daisies and thrift stores

#5338 cut flowers from my garden

#6942 watching my son play baseball

#8156 holding my husband's hand

#10,978 picking blueberries

#13,888 a text from my son in college

#15.098 the sound of our clothes washing

#17,000 beautiful fall leaves

#17,167 the perfect song at the perfect time

Remembering and recording—this is how I fight hard against the enemy's plot to destroy me. When circumstances cloud heavy around my heart and bullies scream loudly, I choose to taste His goodness. I choose to see that the Lord has been good.

*Surely goodness and love will follow me all the days of*
   *my life.*

— PSALMS 23:6

All the days of my life, God's love and His goodness are chasing me down. His goodness is coming for me. It's coming for you too.

Sometimes that means happy-as-can-be, things-are-just-how-we-want-them kind of good. The "all is well" kind of good. Everyone is happy, there are no irritations, no stressors, and no mean people. All the laundry is washed *and* put away. The dishwasher is empty and so is the sink. The kids are good. All of them at the *same* time. No mice in the house. No weeds in the garden. No errands to run. No security tag left on the shirt I just bought. No teeth with cavities needing filled. The bills are paid. The taxes are done. I still fit in my favorite pair of jeans. We have money to update our outdated house. Diet Coke won't give me cancer. The vehicles are running. The roof doesn't leak. A clearance sale is happening at TJ Maxx . . . .

My husband and I were on our nightly walk one evening recently when I stopped abruptly and said, "Hey Babe! Everything is good! Everyone is good! Stop, let's soak this moment in. Honey, how about we just don't go home. Let's just keep walking in this rare *all is well* moment . . . ."

But we did have to go back home.

If I see God's goodness on different terms, it blows open a new way of living that looks less like barely surviving and more like thriving once again. It's the fresh breath of air this worn out girl desperately needs.

So how about giving it a shot with me?

It's really not hard. You'll see.

Mornings when your burdens are light and stress is low: Goodness.

Just the right verse on a morning when you're discouraged: Goodness.

Sun shining: Goodness.

Rain watering my flowers so I don't have to: Goodness.

A $50.00 bouquet of flowers: Goodness.

Wildflowers picked from the side of a road: Goodness.

Healthy kids: Goodness.

Precious snuggle time when the kids aren't feeling well: Goodness.

Provision for the thing you really want: Goodness.

Contentment when you have less: Goodness.

A vacation with your man: Goodness.

A stroll in the neighborhood park with that same man: Goodness.

When your kid makes the team or wins the scholarship: Goodness.

Profound life lessons gained when they do not: Goodness.

Now you give it a whirl!

Where is there goodness in your life?

I think we all have noticed that we live in an increasingly hard to please, highly critical, seldom ever satisfied culture. We expect everything from half time shows to Easter services to get more impressive year to year. We anticipate bigger vacations. We expect to see substantial growth in our investments. We want increasing status and stuff. We desire ease. We want blessings—big ones, preferably. The problem is that this isn't necessarily how it works in God's economy. It certainly wasn't the life Jesus or his followers had while they walked these earthly streets of dust in their knock off versions of Birkenstocks. Life didn't increasingly get easier, peachier or better.

God told it to us straight up. He said we *will* have trouble in this world (John 16:33).

Suffering is normal. Suffering should be expected. Suffering should stop being a surprise to us. Life is good, and at the same time, suffering comes standard issue with our baby certificate. It's wise to accept both. The most influential people who have ever lived suffered greatly. You really wouldn't want a life of ease. Depth of character and depth with Jesus are forged in suffering. I want both. You do too even if you are wondering if that makes suffering worth it. Take it from a middle aged woman: Yes, it makes suffering worth it. God has used it all to grow *beautiful* things in my life. And in yours too. Dirt is needed to grow flowers you know.

The more *grown up* and *beautiful* we become, we actually are more impressed with less. Have you noticed that? We begin to have eyes to perceive the least of things as blow you away impressive touches of God's goodness. We see goodness every-where, even in disappointments. The silver lining is easier to recognize. We are thrilled more easily. We clap with greater enthusiasm. The critic in us diminishes. We find our childlike awe once again. We give God fewer ultimatums. This is what happens to us as we *grow up* instead of *growing old*. Redefine goodness so you can begin to see it. Then be prepared to be impressed.

Did you know that God invites us to taste and see that He is good (Psalm 34:8)? Taste God's goodness at your next meal. You have the ability to make dinner because of hands that work and eyes that see. Wow, what a blessing! As much as I loathe cook-ing, I should be blown away that I have the ability and the finan-cial provision to prepare a meal for my family. Even if I do royally stink at it.

Taste that coffee each morning. God made you coffee beans. I repeat. God made coffee beans! Oh glory be to God. That's His love and mercy right there. And pineapple. Are you serious? My mouth literally gets so excited. Raspberries. Are they not the cutest things ever?

We literally have the privilege of tasting God's goodness. Ten thousand taste buds just so we can enjoy food. Wowzers! God is so good to us.

See it in a friendly face on a particularly lonely day. See it in your kids walking in the door after school. See it in your husband's eyes just for you. The mountains that belong to God, the seas that He gathers up in jars, the sunsets He paints, the stars He calls out each night by name, the grass that grows faithfully along with those cute-as-a-button yellow dandelions. Seriously, dandelions! They are God's absolutely free, zero maintenance, always come back even after you mow over them gifts for us to enjoy. Young kids delight greatly in picking them as their very first present for their mommies. Maybe consider leaving a few in your yard for the little ones in your neighborhood.

His goodness is chasing you down all the days of your life.

Start recording, you'll see.

The old stuff I rescued on the farm that day? Well, I placed the old metal mailbox on our patio. It's home to my gardening tools. The white chippy window frame sits on our fireplace mantel. The tin milking buckets now hold rich soil for summer flowers. I wiped off the dirt built up from years of neglect. I gave them another chance and gave them a new purpose. I searched for these treasures; when I found them, I brought them home, washed them off, and gave them a place again.

That's what God has done for me and what He wants to do for you.

You are not tossed aside, sweet one. God desires to restore you too. He has made His way down that dusty country road because He is *that* good and He loves you *that* much. He is coming for you. I'm certain of that. He has plopped down right next to you alongside that dilapidated barn. He knows you have been beat up. He knows you feel unworthy. He knows that you feel lonely. He is placing His hand on your knee and looking your way with a big smile. With bright, caring eyes He says:

"Sweet girl, how 'bout it? Ready to get outta here? I'm ready to rescue you. Whaddya say?"

———

P.S. If you have been wounded by the church and you subsequently gave up on God or His Church as a result, please hear me. I am so sorry. I understand how painful that kind of wounding is. We didn't go to church for two months after a certain hurt. Honestly, I loved the break. It's easier not to go, isn't it? But this is what I'm certain of: We can't find complete healing or fulfillment apart from the body of Christ. Find a new church if need be. But don't stay away from God's church because the people in it failed you. If we can enter church ready to fixate on who God is rather than who wounded us, our peace will return.

It wasn't easy but I did find courage to go back to church. I was so scared I had full on panic attacks at first when I entered the building. I turned around and walked right back to my van a couple of times just to gather myself and breathe before heading back in to try again. Eventually my feelings caught up with my decision to get back in there. I'm glad I did. You will be too. And you know what? The reality is, most of the time, we're all doing the best we know how to do. We all love Jesus. We all make mistakes. We all carry around our past and our pain. When I began to see the people who hurt me as simply people with their own stories and background, it made it easier for me to find courage. We have an enemy and it isn't flesh and blood. Don't let the devil convince you otherwise.

———

## CHOOSING SWEETNESS: GOING DEEPER WITH GOD

*Being confident of this: that He who began a good work in you will carry it on to completion until the day of Christ Jesus.*

— PHILIPPIANS 1:6

*I have loved you with an everlasting love; I have drawn you with unfailing kindness.*

— JEREMIAH 31:3

*I have seen his ways, but I will heal him; I will guide him and restore comfort to him, creating praise on the lips of the mourners.*

— ISAIAH 57:18-19

*Even though someone is pursuing you to take your life . . . (you) will be bound securely in the bundle of the living by the Lord your God.*

— 1 SAMUEL 25:29

*Look to the Lord and His strength. Seek His face always. Remember the wonders He has done.*

— PSALM 105:4-5

*Let us not give up meeting together, as some are in the
habit of doing, but let us encourage one another . . . .*

— HEBREWS 10:25

- Do you feel tossed aside? If so, why?
- Do you see yourself as worthy of a rescue? Why or why not?
- What would it mean for you and look like in your life for you to be restored?
- Have you given up on church because of hurt? Would you consider asking God to give you the courage and perspective needed to go back?
- Buy yourself a journal and start counting the ways. I can't think of a better gift for your family than finding journals one day packed full of the gifts God gave you along the way.

---

SWEET NUGGETS: TAKEAWAYS TO REMEMBER

*If someone didn't design you, they don't get to define you.*

*Remembering and recording is how you can fight hard against the enemy's plot to destroy you.*

*Even when people are not good to you, God has been.*

*Suffering should not be a surprise.*

*We can't find healing and wholeness apart from the body of Christ.*

*The more grown up we are the more we are impressed with less.*

16

## HIS BELOVED

*I* saved the most important thing—*the very best thing*—for last.

More than anything, I want you to remember this:

You are God's beloved.

He is quite smitten with you. I imagine him leaning over to his angels in heaven and declaring (a little too loudly): "Hey Guys! See her? That one right there? She's mine! Ain't she something?!"

He adores you as you are. Did you know that? In your mess, dysfunction, heartaches, habits, doubts, wounds, burdens, fears, disappointments—all of it. He loves you still. He can't help himself. He made you. He sees you. He cares about you. And He is the one who totally gets you. *He's got you.* Okay?

If you forget everything else in this book, that's fine. No biggie. Just promise me you will start living like you know you're loved. You must recommit to behave like you know both *who* you are and *whose* you are.

My husband asks our teenage girls those questions every night as he tucks them into bed, "Do you know who you are and whose you are? You must know it!" He gently taps them on the forehead while he speaks over them. This loving father is desperate for his daughters to absolutely solidify that truth in their precious minds. Our Abba Father feels the same.

*The beloved of the Lord rest secure in Him, for He*
*shields (her) all day long and the one the Lord loves*
*rest between His shoulders.*

— DEUTERONOMY 33:12

The beloved of the Lord gets to rest secure. We *get* to. Oh, how I want that.

We get to ride across Jesus's shoulders like a sheep every time we are weary or wounded. Just tug at Jesus's hand and say the word. He will hoist you up on His broad shoulders so you can rest for a while. He won't mind a bit. He may even have a granola bar in His shirt pocket to share with you too.

Rest secure with Him. He's got you. And you have Him.

When pressure mounts, when people are mean, when stress increases, when there seems to be no way out, when a crisis hits and bullies roam free, you get to be secure in your God. He loves you enough to offer that to you as you bundle yourself up in Him. I'd suggest we take Him up on the offer.

Did you know that in your darkest, ugliest moments you can still rest secure in His love? God doesn't love you one iota less in those times than He does when you're behaving your cute little self. Like when you're managing to not lose your cool with your kiddos in the grocery store or even showing some serious self-restraint when shopping Hobby Lobby's 50% off aisles. (Nice work by the way, girlfriend.)

He loves you perfectly when you're not perfect.

A friend of mine told me about her bedtime routine with her three-year-old, Anna. Every night she would say, "Mommy loves you," and her little girl would respond, "I wike (like) you, Mommy."

Weeks went by with this bedtime routine. My friend began to wonder why Anna would not say, "I love you," rather than just "I wike you." It was beginning to concern her mama's heart. One night, inadvertently, my friend departed from her normal verbiage and said:

"I like you, Anna."

Anna sat straight up, her eyes widened, and, with great enthusiasm, she declared:

"You mean you wike me and you wove me, Mommy?"

"Yes, honey, I like you and I love you."

That's how God feels about you! He loves you *and* He likes you—so very much.

God likes you.

Read that again. Marinate on it for a moment longer.

He enjoys your company. He gets excited about spending time with you. He looks forward to it. He is thrilled when you talk to Him, worship Him and think about Him. It literally makes His day. You delight Him so much when you choose to spend time hanging out together, just the two of you.

> *The Lord your God is with you; He is mighty to save.*
> *He will take great delight in you. He will quiet you*
> *down with His love, He will rejoice over you with*
> *singing.*
>
> — ZEPHANIAH 3:17

His love quiets you down. I can't get over how precious that is. You will be okay—Daddy is here. Precious sisters in Christ, we were created to be quieted down in our Father's love. No matter what is revving us up, His love quiets down our sweet minds and hearts.

If we miss this, we miss the way out of the pit, out of defeat and on our way towards true *beauty*. We don't stand a chance without remaining planted in God's love. Our joy, security and calmness are tied to it.

It doesn't matter a hill of beans who doesn't treat you like you're loved. God does. Period. So, there! The fat lady just sang. At the end of the day, you go to bed loved. Everyone else's love is the extra icing but it is not the cake. The cake and the icing is me and my Jesus. I'm safe with Him.

If I believe that I am deeply loved, that I am God's beloved girl who gets to be secure, who gets to be bound up in His bundle, who gets to be calmed down when life is revving me up; then even if my husband fails me or my boss or my BFF or church leaders or whoever it might be, it doesn't matter. I am already secure.

There is no other soul on this planet that can do that for you. No one should. No one can. No one is equipped for *that* kind of job in your life. Victorious Christian living is only possible if you're basking in and remaining in Jesus's love for you.

There is no formula for this. It's a state of being. It's a mental framework. It's a filter that sifts through the muck. A lens through which we process life. A pattern of choosing how to think.

As I get ready to say goodbye to you my precious sojourner and friend, I want to leave you with some thoughts I wrote before our last move. I wrote this prayer right before we made it public that we were leaving. An hour after we placed that dreaded For Sale sign in our front yard we got a call from the couple who would end up buying our home (the couple I didn't want to meet, remember).

You know the ending to that story. We asked for a miracle that our home would sell quickly. Considering the housing market in our community, a miracle is what we would need to sell our home at all. I sensed God said He would do it and then

He actually did but I didn't know the ending when I wrote this prayer. We never do know our endings when God invites us to trust Him in the beginning. I'm learning to not wait for hindsight to walk in peace.

Here's what I wrote:

Hi God,

Sometimes it hurts because I thought you'd come through like I wanted you to. Like I knew you could. Like I thought you would. But you didn't. So many times you've hurt my feelings. I still believe you. I still love you. I still know you're God but each time . . . something threatens to chip away at my courage. My courage to keep asking and keep believing because what if I'm disappointed, rejected and turned down? Again. Can my heart take anymore? Disillusionment is kicking at my door. Skepticism wants to be my roomie. Cynicism promises to be my bestie. I actually consider it some days. I do.

But I don't want to live like that. I want to trust you when my heart is disappointed. I want to believe that you actually love me even when it sure doesn't seem like you do. So today I kick disillusionment back in the gut. I unfriend cynicism without apology and I tell skepticism to take a hike. A long one. I muster the courage to believe and receive from you, my Abba Father.

Fully, without regard for the perpetual "what ifs." Without trying to guard my heart from you of all things. I'm sorry that I do that to you. I'm sure that hurts your feelings. I'm sorry for making you sad.

I won't hold back this time just because fear tells me that it's just too good to be true. And that God doesn't like to be good to me anyway.

Father, I believe you really will delight us with this one. I believe you're going to answer this prayer just how we have asked. Just like I know you can.

I risk my heart with you. I cry tears of gratitude freely, not worrying if the jokes going to be on me. I receive what I believe you're currently saying to me. Before you prove it I say thank you for what is yet to be because right now I sense you saying it will be. I thank you for your gift of kindness and graciousness and love. I'm overwhelmed by you and all of this. I see no evidence but I'm behaving like you've already given it. I think you like it that I'd ask you for something big. Because you are big.

Love,

Amy Joy

Why? Why risk it? Why not wait until I know that it's real? That it's in the bag before I praise Him and enjoy the thing? Why put my heart on the line with God, again?

I'll tell you why. Because I don't want to miss it, this tender time with my Father. This adventure called life with Him. Crying tears of gratefulness not over what I can see, but over what I have yet to see. This *is* doing the thing with God—the real thing with God. I wouldn't miss it for the world.

This is Him inviting me into this scary, vulnerable place. These are the *sweetest* moments. This is where depth is forged. This is where my roots grow deep and well-nourished. This is where I delight His socks off. This is where the rubber meets the road. This is how I honor Him.

I want God to know I love Him. I want Him to know He can trust me. At some point in our walk with God we need to make this shift. At some point I should be done asking the same old questions. I should know by now He loves me. I should know by now that I can trust Him. The question is, can He say the same of me?

What if I'm wrong about the things I'm believing that God is going to do? Then I'm wrong—that's it. That's the worst thing that can happen.

Recently my husband and I were believing God for something important in the life of one of our kids. We thought God was going to answer our request. But just yesterday the disappointment came. God didn't answer our prayer the way we were so hoping He would and knew that He could.

So, you know what I did? I took a courageous, deep breath, let it go, let God heal my broken heart, and we continued on. We have been there and done that a time or two (or make that a dozen) and look, I'm still breathing, aren't I? This girl is still breathing and loving her Jesus through all life's disappointments. So are you.

He and I are doing life together no matter what. I know full well He is proud of me and delighted that I had childlike faith and took a risk with Him. He loves when I ask big things of Him because He knows I know my Daddy is big and He can do big things. So why not ask? It delights Him so. Don't worry about guarding your heart from Him. He's got your heart. If you can trust Him to heal your heart when it gets broken you will be free to ask Him for big things.

I don't know what it is for you. But can I encourage you to not be afraid? Go there with your Father. Go to that *sweet* place of relationship. Get it all. He may not give you all that you thought you wanted. He might even give you a few things you were certain you didn't want. But through it all you can rest secure. You're loved by the One who thought you up and knit you together. Get all God has for you, dear one. No holding back, okay? He's got you, remember? You're going to be okay.

We can emerge through painful places more *beautiful* and more *grown up* than we ever would have been without them. We are blessed. So very blessed.

Remember to count the ways, okay? We forget sometimes. Heaviness dulls our senses and our memories of all the blessings God has poured out to us before. Your life has *sweet* places— places oozing with *sweetness*, in fact.

And those *bitter* places? God wants to use them for good too. *Sweetness* can emerge through it all.

*Beauty* really can win.

I'll look forward to bumping into you on the *sweet* road, friend. You're far too *beautiful* to choose the *bitter* one, you know. *Ugly* is easy. *Beauty* is not. I want *beauty*. I think you do too.

———

## CHOOSING SWEETNESS: GOING DEEPER WITH GOD

*He heals the brokenhearted and binds up their wounds.*

— PSALM 147:3

*Praise the Lord oh my soul, and forget not all His benefits, who forgives all your sins and heals all of your diseases, who redeems your life from the pit and crowns you with love and compassion, who satisfies your desires with good things so that your youth is renewed like the eagles.*

— PSALMS 103:1-5

———

## SWEET NUGGETS: TAKEAWAYS TO REMEMBER

*God likes me and He loves me.*

*I can live like I know I'm loved.*

*The worst thing that can happen is that I am wrong and then God and I go on together still.*

*God loves to invite me into vulnerable places with him. Depth is forged in those beautiful places where I learn to risk my heart with Him.*

*You're far too beautiful to choose the bitter road.*

*Ugly is easy, beauty is not. I want beauty.*

# EPILOGUE

*I* usually get teary when I close the cover for the last time of a Bible study or a book that I have connected with. I don't want to say goodbye. I'm on the other end this time with the same tears.

I wish I knew your story. I wonder what's on your heart and what you're in the midst of. I want so badly for you to bypass all the hard stuff of life—I do. I want you to be spared from heartache and headaches. But then again I want you to experience God with a depth that only comes walking hand in hand with Him through the *bitter* places.

Many years have passed since I penned some of these chapters. I made the decision long ago that *sweetness* is where I want to head and that *growing up* is the way I want to age. *Ugly* isn't worth it even though it is easier.

I stand at the corner of *bitter* and *sweet* every single day—many times a day, to be precise. Sometimes I still choose the *bitter* road, but I lose my peace every time I do. I still have to choose what I want more of in my life and who I want to become and where I want to end up. Every new day and every new season of my life is a new opportunity for me to make an important decision. To walk down the road to *sweetness* even though I still walk through *bitter* places. I spent over a decade of my life in a fight or flight response. God taught me I have one more option: freedom. I finally decided to take Him up on the offer.

Jesus proclaims:

> *The Spirit of the Sovereign Lord is on me because the*
> *Lord has anointed me to preach good news to the*
> *poor. He has sent me to bind up the brokenhearted,*
> *to proclaim freedom for the captives . . . to comfort*
> *all who mourn and provide for those who grieve . . .*
> *to bestow on them a crown of beauty instead of*
> *ashes, the oil of gladness instead of mourning and a*
> *garment of praise instead of the spirit of despair.*
>
> — ISAIAH 61:1-3A

Jesus was anointed to bind up your precious little heart. How extremely kind is that? He came to set you free from what holds you captive—the labels you've worn, the hurts, the wrongs, the pain, the mistakes you've made, and the heartache you carry.

Jesus came here to earth so that you would know that through Him it is possible for you to be free from it all. It's possible for your broken heart to be bound up and actually healed. It really is possible. Rush to Jesus like Martha did. Spend time with Him, get in His Word, and worship Him. Find a good mentor, get a counselor if needed, stay in church, keep your heart in a posture that's teachable and willing to receive. He will take you on a journey of healing up your heart if you will let Him. The question is never *if* God is able to make a miracle out of us. The question is always will we *let* God make a miracle out of us. Let Him, my friend.

Jesus wants to give you a crown of beauty instead of ashes. What girl doesn't like a little bling now and then? That sounds like a fantastic exchange: my ashes for His *beauty*. And a crown to boot!

There's a catch, though: I must be willing to leave my ash heap. People in biblical times used ashes as a symbol of grieving. They would sit in ash heaps or dump ashes over their heads to symbolize the grief they were experiencing. We do the same sometimes, don't we? We want everyone to know the pain we are in; which is why invitations to pity parties are plentiful. We like the attention. It defines us and we are afraid to leave. Who are we without the ashes? We are comfortable in the heap because we know what to expect. Sympathy and self-pity become faithful familiar companions.

If I want the exchange Jesus offers I have to decide to get up out of the ash heap so I can receive this wonderful gift. I alone will decide how badly I want the beauty over the ashes. I will cooperate or I won't. I will take Him up on His kind offer or I won't. I don't need to make this more complicated than it is.

Jesus offers us the oil of gladness instead of mourning. But I have to sit still long enough to let that soothing oil of gladness wash over me. I imagine this oil pouring out as I kneel before him. Psalm 3 tell us that God is the lifter of our faces. He cups my chin while nudging it towards Him. He says, "Look at me, Amy." He locks eyes with mine. He smiles and begins to pour. I must be patient and still in His presence for this exchange. Will I?

He gives us garments of praise instead of the spirit of despair. Oh, how I love a new outfit, especially one I score from a consignment shop. Wearing praise like a garment is some-thing I desire more than anything. Sometimes despair clings heavy on me. But I want this new garment, which means I must surrender the rags of despair. They are comfy—I'll give them that. Like giving up a well-worn sweatshirt that feels like a faithful friend but looks tired and pitiful, I must surrender what isn't working. I must surrender the rags of despair. Jesus is telling me, "Hand them over, Amy. Give it up so you can put on this gorgeous garment of praise. It'll look good on you. Trust me."

Accept what Jesus wants to give you, okay? Let go of the old, comfortable ways. Keep choosing *sweet* over *bitter*, *beauty* over *ugly, and growing up* over *growing old*. I'm right here with you making the same choice everyday too. You're not alone, precious friend.

Oh, and I can't forget to tell you that I kicked my Diet Coke love affair during the writing of this book! (I know, right?) It was an acquired taste, mind you, but I have now fallen hard for unsweetened sparkling La Croix. See, miracles do happen!

On top of that, I now also drink my coffee straight up black. No more "fu-fu" needed to please this palette. It's actually symbolic to the serious number God did on me during the writing of this book. That's a good thing, I guess you could say. It wasn't easy, but we already know that good hardly ever means easy, does it?

Now let's go live loved, *beautiful*, and free . . . .


With a bundle of love and appreciation for you, your friend and fellow traveler on this foreign soil until we get to go home . . . .

Amy Joy

# ACKNOWLEDGMENTS

To Cory: You have been so good to me. I would not be me without you. I feel most happy, secure, and free when I'm in your arms. Being the woman at your side is my favorite thing— like ever. I love calling you my man. I could not have written this book without your support and your constant nudges. You believed in me before I believed in myself. You've been the wind beneath my wings. I feel blessed to belong to you and am grateful I get to do life with you.

To Drew, Alexis, and Allie Joy: The three of you are hands down my most favorite people on the planet. I like being in your space best of all. Being your mom has been the biggest thrill of my life. You are my most important and satisfying work. I am so happy that I can seriously call each of you my friend. You were the deepest motivation for me to write this book because I want you and your own families one day to know how good God is in the midst of the tough stuff of life. It delights my heart that each of you love Jesus like you do. It's a great day to be Drew! I pick you, Alexis! I love you to the moon and back, Allie!

To Faye, Dorothy and Julie: God graciously gave me each of you. Three different churches, three different states, three different women. You've each been the big sister to me that I so desperately needed in each place we have lived. Thank you for being a safe place for me, for investing in me, for welcoming me when I was new, for making room for me in your already full circle of friends.

To my family—all of you—the Foty, Jefferson, Stout, and Loewen sides: The greatest sacrifice, by far, to this pastorate life is missing you. I would have loved to have raised my kids and lived my adult life near all of you. My heart literally aches sometimes over all that we have missed by not being closer to you. But we have all of heaven, right? I love you. You each mean so much to me.

To the churches we have called home, BAC, ACV, CHAC, and LSCC: Thank you for the privilege of serving alongside you. It hasn't always been easy but nothing worthwhile ever is. You shaped us. You grew us. You welcomed us. We are grateful that our life's journey allowed us to make a pit stop with you.

To the entire SPS Community, my editor, Nancy, and my coach, Marcy : I could not have done this without you. Thank you for your encouragement and constant support in seeing this through.

# ABOUT THE AUTHOR

Amy Joy Stout is a grateful mom of three young adults and a preacher's wife who is crazy about her man. She finds her security in one beautiful and unchanging thing: She is God's beloved.

God has given her a desire and calling to passionately and practically speak God's truth into the lives of women.

Amy speaks at conferences across the country with the desire to encourage people's hearts, inspiring them to live fully and freely. Amy is also a spiritual life and mental vibrancy coach. To invite Amy to speak at your next event or to inquire about coaching services, you may contact her at amy@amystout.org or visit www.amystout.org.

Amy, along with her teaching pastor husband, Cory, also speak as a team at ministry staff conferences, family camps, and marriage retreats. They would consider it an honor and privilege to serve you.

facebook.com/amystoutspeaker

Made in USA - Kendallville, IN
59463_9781733322119
01.18.2024 1327